BLUE DAYS AT SEA

I will make you brooches and toys for your delight
Of bird-song at morning and star-shine at night.
I will make a palace fit for you and me,
Of green days in forests and blue days at sea.

ROBERT LOUIS STEVENSON.

BLUE DAYS AT SEA

AND OTHER ESSAYS

BY

H. V. MORTON

THIRD EDITION

METHUEN & CO. LTD.
36 ESSEX STREET W.C.
LONDON

First Published . October 20th 1932
Second Edition . December 1932
Third Edition . 1932

PRINTED IN GREAT BRITAIN

TO
ALL WHO SERVE
ON THE
HIGH SEAS

CONTENTS

ABOUT MEN

ABOUT WOMEN

ABOUT PLACES

ABOUT MEN

A VISIT TO THE NAVY

I. THE FLEET AT ANCHOR

I

ONCE A year the Lords of Admiralty permit men with pens and typewriters to 'proceed' to the least accessible part of this island to join the Atlantic, or Home, Fleet, as it is now called. They do so in the amiable assumption that once a year the taxpayer may care to know something about the Navy. The men with pens and typewriters are heartily welcomed by the Navy because they have two legs, which are capable of being pulled together or separately.

The formal act of 'proceeding'—and, as memory tells us, the Services never 'go' anywhere except on leave—induces in the civilian a grave and apprehensive frame of mind. Boys proceed to a new school, soldiers proceed to a new battalion, convicts probably proceed to gaol ; and every one of us proceeds from the cradle to the grave. It is a solemn and official method of transit. So you may imagine me, slightly cowed, taking my place in the train to Scotland and carrying in my pocket a brief note from the Admiralty authorizing me to 'proceed' to Invergordon, there to join H.M.S. *Impenetrable*.

Eighteen hours later I stepped out, pale and shattered, on a bleak railway platform. I had no

3

idea where to go or what to do. I imagined myself stopping strangers with the fatuous question :
' Please can you direct me to H.M.S. *Impenetrable ?*',
like a countryman asking the way to the British
Museum. There was no sign of the *Impenetrable*.
There was nothing but bleakness, wind, gaunt
hills, and a promise of salt waters.

' Sir ! ' said a sweet soprano voice at my elbow.

I turned to acknowledge the salute of an
embryonic admiral, who wore the Eton jacket of
a midshipman. The child was regarding me with
the non-committal, half-amused scrutiny which
the Navy bestows on the unfamiliar. He explained—still standing to attention—that he had
been detailed to guide me to H.M.S. *Impenetrable*,
and that the two hefty and experienced Marines
looming obediently in the background were there
to carry my ' gear '.

We set off, the child and I, down the stony high
street. He represented the gigantic machine in
which I was about to submerge myself, and,
despite the difference in our years, I felt respect
and curiosity. I told him that I had never
been on (he looked at me sharply, and I said
' in ') a battleship in my life.

' Really, sir ! ' he remarked, with a glance
which said : ' What strange fish is here ! '

I said that I was prepared to be not only interested but also thrilled. I said that no doubt life
in the Navy was intensely interesting. He said that
it was not too dusty. Then, turning a corner near
the jetty, we came on the amazing sight of the

4

Atlantic Fleet riding at anchor in Cromarty Firth.

The centre of the firth was occupied by immense battleships anchored at regular intervals one from the other, each one to my eye exactly like her sister, but the child said :

'There is the Flagship, *Nelson*. This is the Second Battle Squadron you see here. The battle cruisers are down there, off Cromarty. They always go there. . . .'

Anchored in the remote distance, and looking like a half-smoked cigarette on the skyline, was a kind of Noah's Ark.

'What', I asked, 'is that extraordinary hulk ? '

'That', replied the child, 'is the *Furious*. Aircraft carrier.'

The big slate-coloured ships, with canvas nose-bags on their guns, rode at anchor, their picket boats puffing beneath the grey cliffs of their hulls. Battleship winked knowingly at battleship. Little signal lamps near the bridges shone in dots and dashes as these monsters spoke to each other.

It was a formidable sight. Although the grey giants appeared to be in a drowsy, even benevo-lent, mood, there was a sinister air of watchfulness about so many thousand tons of steel lying at anchor, drawn together from the line of sea and sky—members of a dangerous family, assembled in due order as a great fleet, and winking furtively to each other through the dusk. I had yet to learn that the things battleships say to each other in harbour have little to do with death and destruction. They run more like this :

' Will you dine with me to-night ? ' The answer is ' W.M.P.' (which means ' with much pleasure ') or ' N.C.D.' (which means ' No can do ').

' Here is our boat,' said the child.

We stepped aboard and set our course towards the immense grey flanks of H.M.S. *Impenetrable*. I climbed the accommodation ladder, lifted my hat to the non-existent crucifix on the quarter-deck (as I had been told to do by a seafaring friend), and was pounced on by a young naval officer, who carried a telescope under his arm. He was the officer of the watch. Part of his duty evidently was to watch for me.

It was that time when the quarter-deck of a battleship—that broad space at the stern inter-rupted by bollards and other grey and knobby obstructions—is dotted by officers, two by two, engaged in the familiar art of ' pacing ' this locality. This consists of a quick march fore and aft, turning together, hands held behind the back or thrust into the pockets of blue jackets. An officer ceased ' pacing ' and shook hands with me.

' I'm the commander. Come along to the Ward Room. You're in number eleven cabin.'

So I entered the strange, interesting community known as H.M.S. *Impenetrable*.

The Ward Room, which is the mess of the senior officers, was an angular apartment beneath the boat-deck. Swinging doors separated the ante-

room from the mess room, in which marine servants in white jackets were setting tables for
dinner. The mind, side-tracked for a moment
by the air of conviviality, was brought sharply
back to the realities by the great girders support-
ing the steel deck above, which rose up, support-
ing the low ceiling and reminding the visitor, in
spite of their white paint, that he was in a man-of-
war. Officers lay about in chairs, engaged in that
gloomy spare-time occupation of the Navy,
re-reading old newspapers and periodicals, while
others stood round enjoying one of the few com-
pensations of commissioned life at sea : excellent
pink gin at uncommercial prices.

I was introduced to a puzzling community—
' Torps ', ' Guns ', ' Schoolie ' and the ' Young
Butcher ' were some of their names. They shook
hands with reserved suspicion. I could tell from
the way they looked at me that I was under
probation. My conduct would soon determine
whether I was a bounder or a decent fellow. In
other words, I was at school again.

' Where have they put you ? ' some one asked.

' I don't know.'

' Number eleven, Chastity Alley,' said the
commander.

This, I gathered, was my address in H.M.S.
Impenetrable.

After several pink gins—which, by the way, are
singularly innocuous—I was told to prepare myself
to meet ' the Skipper '. This was the first time
I was made aware of the remote and god-like pres-

ence which presides over His Majesty's ships—the Captain.

It seems, possibly because we are so familiar with the rank of army captain, that a commander should be superior to a captain. It sounds a more impressive rank. But a few minutes in a battle-ship prove that this is not so. A commander spends his life in the fear that he may never be a captain; that an ungrateful Admiralty may regret that there is no ship for him to captain, and so ' axe ' him, which means that he is decanted with an inadequate pension on civil life with no commercial assets but good manners. As so many successful people in commercial life have no manners at all, this is not a very cheerful prospect.

The captain of a battleship is its god. It is sur-prising that a human being can achieve such an air of aloof omnipotence in the confined quarters of any ship. An enormous gulf separates him from even the Ward-Room officers. He may occasionally embarrass every one by dropping in for a glass of sherry, but his life is spent in his own quarters and a sentry of Marines with side arms—a relic of the times when armed men guarded the officers from the fury of the lower deck—stands guard over his exalted privacy.

His quarters were rather like a suite in the Berkeley : a cabin, a private bathroom and a huge dining-room occupying the stern of the ship, gaily furnished with chintz-covered chairs, a grand piano and engravings of naval battles.

A steward in a white jacket came in with a

cocktail shaker. The captain hoped that I was comfortable. We talked about the battle of Trafalgar. The commander rose. I gathered that the audience was over :

'Will you dine with me some night ? '

We went out. I felt rather as Moses must have felt when he came down from Sinai :

'White tie or black ? ' I whispered to the commander.

'I don't understand.'

'When this dinner comes off ...'

'Oh ; tails,' said the commander solemnly.

I felt chastened and rebuked. There was something shocking even in the thought that a man might dine with the captain in a dinner jacket.

II

Now, getting the hang of a battleship and its varied inhabitants is a most puzzling occupation for a civilian.

You must imagine me finding my way to Cabin eleven up staircases, down staircases, slipping, stumbling, getting lost, hitting my head on steel hatchways and iron pipes, arriving on the quarter-deck like a lost rabbit, bolting down again, all in a futile attempt to discover the whereabouts of the elusive place known familiarly as 'Number Eleven, Chastity Alley'. I tracked it down at last.

The cabin contained a bunk, a wardrobe, a

desk, a washing-stand, a mirror, several electric
lights, and a private of Marines (a native of
Tottenham), who had spread out my ' gear ' for
dinner.

We discussed the presence of Royal Marines
in his Majesty's ships, a custom of remote
antiquity :

' We can do everything the Army can do and
everything the Navy can do,' said he modestly.

' Kipling called you ruddy harumphrodites, I
believe.'

' Did he ? ' said the Marine. ' Seven o'clock
tea in the morning, sir ? Very good, sir.'

And he departed, a bulky figure with tattooed
forearms, a grey issue shirt and blue slacks with
a line of red piping down them ; and with him
departed also a vague and improbable atmosphere, almost as though a service flat in St. James's
Street had run away to sea.

We dined cheerfully, and at the end of dinner,
after the port had gone round, we toasted the
King sitting.

' One of the Georges was dining aboard a
man-o'-war,' I was told, ' and when the Ward
Room rose to drink his health a tall man cracked
his head on a wooden beam, so His Majesty very
kindly forbade the Navy to rise for the King.'

We had barely finished dinner before the
commander, who is the matron of a ship, pulled
down his waistcoat, stood up and said :

' " Rounds "—like to come with me ? '

I learnt that when the ' Last Post ' sounds from

the flagship, commanders say good night to their crews.

Waiting for us outside the Ward Room was a Marine bugler with the master-at-arms, who carried a ship's lantern with a candle inside it. This lantern and its candle delighted me. It is a touching survival in a ship which uses electricity as a tennis club uses water.

The bugler went first, blowing a single note— G—on his bugle. The master-at-arms followed, and the commander brought up the rear.

A battleship at night is a queer, stuffy place. Hammocks slung from hooks festoon the ship in every direction, so that the commander walks quickly in a stooping position. It is strange, too, that a modern battleship at night, with its swinging brown hammocks, should in some strange way resemble its forefather, the wooden ship. The hammocks hide the white steel girders, you forget the machinery ; you grope round in a dim light, and it occurs to you that you might be making an inspection of the old *Victory*.

The master-at-arms swings the candlelight in dark corners as you go on down narrow steel alley-ways. When the ship's company hear the bugle they come to attention. You pass through the hot breath of the ship's galleys. More men at attention. You enter dark, eerie corners, where ghostly electric blue lamps shine above the hammocks. You dodge left and right to avoid these hammocks ; and so, at length, you emerge again in the Ward Room.

'Rounds' have been completed. H.M.S. *Impenetrable* is officially kissed and tucked up for the night !

If you listen you will hear the clatter of hard boots on steel plates, the confusion of a thousand loud-voiced seamen entering their swinging beds. Then enforced silence ; and the ship sleeps. . . .

The master-at-arms opens the lantern and blows out the candle. So the Navy goes to bed each night much as its great-grandfather did in the days of the wooden walls.

III

After rounds, while some played cards, some talked, and a few continued to re-read *The Times* and to gaze again at pictures of last week's bride in the *Tatler*, the commander said suddenly to me :

'Come along and meet the Gun Room.'

The Gun Room is the midshipman's retreat.

The midshipman is unfailingly popular in civil life, especially on the music hall when he is interpreted by girls with improbable curves. In the Navy he is a kind of fag. He is linked by birth and destiny to his superior officers, yet he is forced to fetch and carry for them. The student of sociology must see in this trim, slight figure a pleasing vindication of that unpopular institution, aristocracy. The lower deck likes the midshipman and, while fully conscious of his defects and shortcomings, respects him as a member of the ruling class. It is always willing to cover up his mistakes. What could be more satisfying to the delicious snobbery of the English democrat than the privilege of protecting the scion of a race of admirals from the fury of a man who will never be more than a commander ?

The Navy, alone of all our national institutions, has discovered the secret of transforming the male cub into a presentable human being at a time in life which is admitted to be both uncomfortable and regrettable. He is neither man nor boy. He is in the between-years when his fellows ashore, suddenly losing their treble voices and becoming conscious of beauty and its dangers, lack direction and example. The Navy cunningly dignifies the midshipman—who is, of course, not a ' man ' at all—with the attributes of manhood and the shadow of authority, so that, catching him during the most impressionable and imitative years of his life, it stamps him for ever, just as the Jesuits stamp their prey. Once a priest, always a priest ; once a midshipman, always a midshipman. This is what women mean when they say that naval officers are so clean and boyish. It also, in part, explains the limitations and prejudices of naval officers, which are those of the schoolroom. Peter Pan is an old fogey compared with a group of naval officers, confronted with an unfamiliar aspect of life. Scratch even an admiral —if any one would dare to do such a thing—and you find a ' snotty ', because some corner of the naval officer's mind is for ever labelled ' Gun Room '.

The Gun Room of a battleship is notorious for frequent outbursts of youthful exuberance, during which an honoured guest may, and generally does, find himself forced to contribute to the kind of entertainment to which he has been a stranger since his undergraduate days. It is all very good-humoured and high-spirited.

The Gun Room of H.M.S. *Impenetrable* was a small room about the size of a suburban drawing-room, but there the resemblance ceased with startling suddenness. My first impression was that, in order to make it fit for future admirals to live in, violent, but entirely successful, battles had been fought with lavatory attendants in every part of the British Isles. 'Wash and Brush Up, 3*d*.', 'Ladies', 'Gentlemen', and other signs hung proudly on the walls in wrought copper, cardboard, and plain enamel.

Three young midshipmen were sitting in the Gun Room—one at a table writing, one full length on an experienced-looking settee, and the third beside an ancient and alcoholic piano which, like all Gun Room pianos, is now and then given a glass of beer just to encourage the poor blighter.

They had, I gathered, just concluded a ' moan '. Now the ' moan ' of a Gun Room is the naval version of an Army ' grouse ', only it is better organized, and is more comprehensive. The midshipmen fling their moanful forms into chairs, and one says :

' Come on, you chaps, let's have a moan ! '

' Well ; my moan is . . .' begins the first, and

14

so they go on in great detail. It is good for the soul : a kind of spiritual emetic.

The unofficial description of a midshipman is : ' A method of conveying abuse from one naval officer to another naval officer of senior rank.'

' I don't understand that,' I said.

' Well, you see, sir, it's like this,' explained a midshipman. ' The captain calls me and he says, " Go and ask Lieutenant Brown what he imagines he's doing with that boat ! " I go and say, " Please, sir, the captain wants to know what you are doing with that boat ! " " Oh," says Lieutenant Brown with unseemly anger, " the answer is—go to hell ! " Then I go back and say, " Mr. Brown says that it's all right, sir, and he'll be off in a second, sir ! " You see the idea . . . ? '

The most absolute autocrat in a ship—after, of course, the captain—is the sub-lieutenant in charge of the Gun Room. Here his word is law. He keeps a cane in his cabin with which he, and he alone, can chastise the budding admirals under his charge.

' Of course, I don't cane one a month,' said this young demi-god to me ; ' but now and then, don't you know, one simply has to prevent them making fools of themselves. Then they get six of the best.'

' Not in the Gun Room ? '

' Good lord, no ; in the bathroom, where you can get a good sweep on.'

' But snotties seem on the whole exceedingly well-mannered and smart.'

'Oh, they're not too bad! Sometimes a new snotty is a bit funny. I remember one little fellow who was told to go and tell an officer that the main derrick was to be worked at six-thirty. "Right-o," said the officer, "let me know when the balloon goes up, will you?" At six-thirty the snotty went up, saluted, and said, "They're working the main derrick, sir, but I can't see the balloon anywhere. . . ."'

The midshipmen sleep amidships in hammocks, or on the deck, wrapped in blankets. One of the great arts in moving about a battleship at night is not to walk on or into the sleeping snotties.

Early in the morning a midshipman, detailed day by day and known as the Duty Snotty, awakens his messmates by the simple act of either kicking them or prodding them. They then awaken like a flock of starlings, chattering as only the very young can chatter at 6.15 a.m., and disappear on deck to be drilled by a Physical Training Instructor or a gunner's mate or to try out their nascent authority on themselves.

In the evening, when dressing for dinner, you can often hear the name of some actress mentioned with devotion, for the Gun Room is subject to 'pashes'. The leader of a 'push' is sometimes sufficiently enterprising to write to the object of the 'pash' and request a signed photograph. This is never refused.

A midshipman receives £7 10s. a month, and his average mess bill is £4 10s. If he is under eighteen, his wine bill for the month is limited to

10*s.* ; over eighteen, he can spend 15*s.* on drink. If he exceeds this, he goes before the captain and knows all about it and, unless he can give adequate reason for his excess, frequently takes the water cure for long, dreary weeks.

In the old days the Gun Room was the scene of wild and violent games, many of them, I believe, brutal. These have gone out of fashion.

' Dogs of War ' is, however, still played.

The sub. in charge of the Gun Room shouts out ' Dogs of War ! ', and his wild young men line up ready to perform outrageous orders.

Before the war the officers of a German battleship dined aboard a British battleship. Things became bright, even brilliant. The German officers stood apart, unable, or unwilling, to join in the fun. The sight of midshipmen waltzing with senior officers offended their sense of propriety. Somehow, towards the murky end of the evening, the captain of the British ship emerged from the undergrowth of a Rugger scrum wearing the jacket of a midshipman, and declaring that never had a better ' rag ' been staged by the Navy since Britannia ruled the waves.

' And you,' said the senior German officer to the British captain, ' you command this ship ? '

' I do,' said the British captain, straightening his midshipman's jacket ; ' and, what's more, I'll race you round the quarter-deck for a fiver.'

The German refused the challenge, and, with a baleful eye on the midshipman's jacket, said :

' And they obey you—*after this ?* '

17

'They damned well do!' said the British captain.

'I don't understand it at all,' mused the German, who departed wrapped in a perfect fog of bewilderment.

IV

I say good night and go upon the quarter-deck. The stars are out. About us I can see the dark shapes of our companion ships, the lights twinkling in them. There is something almost terrifying in so much power lying still in the night with the stark hills round them. There is the sound of a motor boat taking a captain back to his ship after a dinner with an even greater than he. It chugs on in a V of pale phosphorescence, and then comes silence. The Fleet is asleep.

I discover the steps that lead down to Chastity Alley. I get lost among gun racks. I try various ladders. I find myself again on the quarter-deck. The Marine sentry outside the captain's quarters kindly tells me the way. I plunge again into the iron depths, but find the outer suburbs, in which Chastity Alley is situated, immensely complicated by sleeping snotties. Hammocks festoon the air. The passages of the Alley look as though hung with cocoons, and each cocoon has the face of a midshipman. I strike a match and, with infinite care, bending my head, tiptoe between them. The match-light falls on their faces. Can these be the smart young almost officers of the Gun Room?

Sleep and pyjamas and tousled hair have turned
them into children. That precocious, manly,
beer-drinking air has departed from them, and
sleep, stripping them of their veneer and their
splendid pretence at manhood, reveals them as
the infants they are. Another match lights me
to No. 11, and just before it dies I see the face
of the child who led me to the Fleet and steered
the picket boat with such confidence, a dirk
swinging jauntily at his hip, towards the steel
flanks of the *Impenetrable*.

No longer does he resemble a budding admiral.
Sleep has reduced him almost to the nursery. I
hate to say it, but his mother, his sisters and even
possibly his aunts, seeing him at that unguarded
moment, would not have treated him as officers
of His Majesty's Navy are treated—at least in
public.

There are some things which a man sees only
once. He may afterwards see them every day of
his life, but never in quite the same way. The
first time you awaken early in a battleship and
go up on deck is one of these moments.

The great ship towers above you in an uncanny
grey light not of sun or moon. It is cold. The
sea is as grey as the sky. Riding lights are still
burning on the ensign and jack staffs. Ahead
and astern lie the ships of the Battle Squadron,
black shadows on grey water—their bridges, their
spotting tops, their guns dark against the thin
red streamers of the dawn. . . .

All round you that mysterious family—the Fleet
—is awakening. In each grey ghost of a ship is
the same dark parade on deck, the same jumble
of sleepy voices, as the seamen whose work, like
a woman's, is never done, prepare to serve their
ship through another twenty-four hours. The
officer of the watch comes up, cold and muffled
to the eyes. He points to a shadow far off down
the Firth.

'Destroyers! See them?'

A fleet is a strange thing. You never actually
see it in the same way that you see an army. Its
area extends over the curve of the earth's surface.
Its members are always slipping away on mysterious errands. The destroyers, like grey cats,
go out on their hunting by night, and early
in the morning you can see them slinking
home again—grey cats that have been out all
night.

Yet you are intensely conscious of the fleet.
Grey masts are always popping up on the skyline. Great grey ships are always lurking round
you. Sometimes a whole squadron crosses our
bows steaming busily on some unknown occasion
—part of us, yet apparently independent of us ;
and the air is stiff with messages that could, if
they would, bring the Navy together from the
edges of the sky.

The ship's company plunge into all kinds of
activity in the morning light. There is an
informal air about it. Men in sweaters come
running round the deck. The commander strides

about, rubber boots on his feet, a woollen muffler about his neck and his telescope under his arm. Suddenly, with nerve-shattering informality, God appears on deck. He is wearing flannel trousers and a sweater. He looks almost like an ordinary human being. Men stiffen at his approach as he goes past, bareheaded and smiling, the sensitive observer realizing with a surge of astonishment that he probably has a private life ashore in which a woman ventures to contradict him. The sight of a battleship's captain in athletic mufti is as embarrassing as it would be to discover the King in his pyjamas. He goes over the side, where a small private pulling boat is waiting to give him early-morning exercise.

Throughout the Fleet the same activities are occurring with mechanical uniformity in each ship. Perhaps on the quarter-deck of the flag-ship the King of the Gods, the Admiral, sweeps a telescope over his armada, noting with approval the perfect pattern of its activity.

The domestic affairs and the official activity of the Army can be kept separate, because there is always a parade ground. The Army is like a man with his own private business life. The Navy, however, is distressingly feminine because the smell of cooking is seldom absent from its solemn moments. Domestic life is always break-ing in. A sailor's work is never done. Men may work, but sailors must sweep. So you will find in the Navy, that while something important is happening on the quarter-deck some one is polishing a piece of brass not far away. Even the Lord God of the Fleet is liable to trip over a man with a scrubbing brush. These intimate activities, which are performed as far as possible by numbers, lend to the Navy a humour and a humanity which is totally lacking in the Army. No man has ever fallen in love with a barracks, but many a man loves his ship.

As the morning advances, bugles sound, Marines fix bayonets, slope arms and march to the quarter-deck with a band. At eight o'clock in the summer, an hour later in winter, a signalman slowly raises the White Ensign on its staff at the stern of the ship. The Marines present arms. The band plays ' God Save the King '. The ship's company ceases to paint the ship, to polish the guns, to scrub the decks. It stands to attention. Over the waters the faint notes of the Anthem are blown from other quarter-decks. All round the White Ensigns take the morning sun. The band then strikes up the ship's march—it may be ' The Farmer's Boy ' or ' For He's a Jolly Good Fellow ' (the tune of ' Malbrouck s'en va-t-en guerre ') or almost anything—and then, ' Colours ' over, the Marines march off, and His Majesty's ship, having saluted His Majesty's flag, goes on painting itself grey outside or white inside. And from galleys comes the sound of intensive cooking !

Breakfast in a Ward Room is recognized to be

a silent occasion. It is sometimes marred by the abnormal and indecent cheerfulness of a man whose rank precludes rebuke.

'Morning, chaps!' he cries, entering like a summer breeze, rubbing his hands together with horrible affability and administering a playful pat to the head of a torpedo officer. Men writhe silently, or shrink away from him, or gaze up bleakly from the *Sketch*, which is propped up before them on the world's most misanthropic invention, a table reading-rack.

After breakfast you carry a cup of tea or coffee into the anteroom. Some one is discussing an inspection of gun turrets. Some one wants something from the paymaster. In the midst of this the surgeon-commander enters and, with the gloomy and anxious face of a mother, says that the ship next door has a suspected case of measles.

You prowl round the newspaper racks, wondering if there is still an advertisement that you have not read. You take up an old copy of the *Tatler* and gaze again on the bride whose face you have seen so often that you feel both married to and divorced from her.

v

A battleship is a steel island crammed with incomprehensible inventions and inhabited by a race of double-jointed men who speak a strange and difficult language. These men spend their lives either painting the island, scrubbing its decks with holystone (known as ' Bibles ') until it looks like the floor of the Albert Hall on a ball night, fussing round the guns with which the island is dotted, nursing the turbines which drive the island through the seas, cooking amazing quantities of food, running up and down apparently perpendicular 4-inch steel stairs in issue boots without arriving in hospital ; and retiring to rest at night in swinging hammocks which during the day—when tied up in bundles—look exactly like the sausages in Soho.

You can, if you know when to turn to the left and when to descend a manhole, find a hot bath or a newly-baked rockcake at any hour of the day or night. There is more electricity in the island than in the Savoy Hotel, and the wires, which are the nerves of the island, are so arranged that if part of the island is shot away by the King's enemies, that part which still remains has enough power to deliver a broad-side and to provide sufficient electric light in which to write home and tell mother all about it.

It is difficult to say which is the most important thing in the island. If we admit that movement is essential to it, we must vote for the 45,000 horse-power turbines, upholstered in unpainted oak, which rise dome-like among the white paint and copper tubes of the engine room. The boilers are so delicate that they drink only distilled water.

The Lieutenant-Commander of Engine Room

Mysteries may often be observed squinting like a chemist at a tube of water into which he has dropped a bead of silver nitrate. If a pale mist forms in the tube the lieutenant-commander frowns and turns small brass wheels, gazing at the same time at appropriate dials! This seems to improve matters! A white mist in the water means that it is good enough for you or me, but is not pure enough for a battleship's boilers.

If the prime object of a battleship is to shoot, undoubtedly its most important objects are the 16-inch guns which expose their gigantic muzzles from grey turrets. When these guns are fired all the pictures have to be taken down from the Ward Room, and every wife is carefully removed from every cabin desk and placed reverently between a packing of pyjamas. Large steel girders are erected to reinforce the decks so that the island may withstand the shock to its nervous system. If, by a piece of good luck, you remain conscious when all nine guns are fired together, your first thought will be that the whole universe has exploded, but second thoughts will convince you that it was only your ear-drums cracking. (But who hit you a violent blow on the back of the head? There is a place low down on the right side which aches for hours after the 16-inch guns have barked!)

The explosion is, in fact, so violent that a battleship, travelling ahead at twelve knots, is said to be displaced a foot to the side—but it feels much worse!

3

After I had lived for some days in one of the outer suburbs of the *Impenetrable*, I had the superficial impression that a tourist might have after a cheap week-end in Paris. But nothing could be less Parisian than the *Impenetrable*.

She was sired by Dreadnought out of Jutland, at a cost of £7,488,274 ! Her nine 16-inch guns and turret armour alone cost £3,000,000. It costs £300 to fire three of her nine 16-inch guns, she carries a crew of about 1,200 men, and, with extreme luck, the thoughtful visitor may be able to find somewhere about her a nut, screw, knob or bolt small enough and humble enough to represent his income tax.

My first impression was that only a frequent tramcar service, an underground railway, a few public houses, and a zoo are necessary to make this ship complete. She has a " town hall ", a concert room, a " law court ", a church, a hospital, an operating theatre, miles of steel streets, shops in which you can find anything from wireless valves to bottles of perfume, bakehouses and kitchens which rival those of the Ritz, a broadcasting station and six telephone exchanges !

Nothing like her has ever sailed the seas. The *Iron Duke* class battleships, which in 1914, when Jellicoe was consul, were the last word in design and death power, are provincial in comparison with these vast, untraditional, steel acres, so full of modern comforts that one forgets they are merely the most powerful mobile gun platforms on earth and, of course, the world's finest monument to the insanity of man.

Large tracts of the *Impenetrable* are still on the secret list, and I was continually being shown things as a taxpayer which I must not reveal as a writer—even if I understood their significance ! It is, however, obvious to any one who explores the *Impenetrable*, deck after deck, that when she was designed Sir Eustace d'Eyncourt, the late Director of Naval Construction, said, ' We will build a battleship that can be bombed, torpedoed four times at once, shot at in sections, mined and otherwise assaulted, without changing expression.'

The *Impenetrable* presents the same kind of problem to an enemy that one of Chubb's toughest safes might present to an optimistic boy with an air gun.

Below decks—as far below as the galley slaves of the Roman triremes—live the 1,200 men. Since the invention of armour plate the life of a battleship has been driven below. I have been told that on extraordinary occasions, when a whole ship's company has come to the surface, men have been surprised by strange, unfamiliar faces. There must be men living secret lives somewhere far down in the depths, probably even preserving their anonymity by drawing their pay by proxy !

It must be difficult, however, in the *Impenetrable*. On every deck are loud speakers. No one can escape them ! All orders filter down to the very depths via the microphone. It is rather amusing to stand on deck and to watch a small Marine bugler open a steel box and blow routine calls into a microphone ! Still stranger is the sight of a man blowing an archaic bo'sun's whistle into it, followed by a command which is broadcast into every nook and corner of the enormous labyrinth.

In the long, steel avenues the men work, eat, and live. There is a room with a piano, in which they can smoke. There are bathrooms with hot and cold water. There are spotless kitchens. There are steam-heated lockers in which food is kept warm. But these men have their moans. No sailor would be normal without a ' moan ' or a soldier without a ' grouse '.

' I thought ', said one ' moaner ', ' that when I joined this ship I should be able to read in bed at last ! You see there's an electric switch near my hammock ; but no such luck ! They turn 'em off from the main switch just like they do in other ships. . . .'

And the surprising thing about the *Impenetrable* is that the men sleep in hammocks ! It would not have surprised me to find them bedded down in dormitories with chintz curtains. But at night they sling their hammocks between decks as if they were in the *Victory*.

As you go down Main Street, past several large and imposing factories, into Marine Square, where rifles stand in racks, you come to a flight of iron steps (or, more nautically, a ladder), which leads you to the church. This is the first battleship church issued by the Admiralty with chairs, altar rail and an altar. (I wonder how that reads in official records : ' Altar, oak, church, for the use of, one ' ?) It is dedicated to St. Christopher.

The strange and interesting thing about St. Christopher's is that if you go there at 6 a.m. you will hear Mass ; if you go at other times you will hear a Protestant service. This is probably the only place of worship in the world where the Catholic lion and Protestant lamb lie down together. The reason is that the church is not consecrated but merely dedicated, and as one officer put it, ' the more prayers said in this world the better.'

' You have been down to the cold storage ? ' asked an officer. ' How interesting ! What is it like ? I'm told we make seventy tons of fresh water a day. Did you see the plant ? I really must go down and have a look some day.'

That is the *Impenetrable*. No one has seen all of her. Even to those living in her and busy with her she is rather like the Tower of London to the Londoner—a place to see some day.

VI

Many people still believe, for tradition dies hard, that the typical sailor—or Jack Tar—is a man with a brown beard who comes ashore smelling of rum and holding a green parrot in a cage. Once on dry land, he is supposed to lurch with a nautical roll into the nearest patch of trouble, and he is described in forthcoming police-court proceedings as ' a sea-faring man of rough appearance '.

This impression is a hundred years out of date. The modern Navy is an electric machine. Our latest ships are fitted with electric bakeries and electric laundries and electric lifts. But the result arrived at by fifty large-boned able seamen pulling together on the same rope is to-day usually achieved by one man pressing a button. The typical modern seaman is a cross between a mechanic and a senior wrangler. In plain clothes he looks like ' something in the City '. When he goes on leave he carries, not a kit-bag, but a green canvas suitcase of a uniform pattern as decreed by my lords of the Admiralty ; and in his spare time he constructs wireless sets and reads books about electricity.

I wonder what Nelson would say to a modern ship's company ! He would not recognize them as sailors. Only about 25 per cent. draw their rum ration : the rest prefer a small allowance in money ! The Higher Educational Test indicates the type of man who is entering the Navy.

If you wander about a battleship between the hours of 5 p.m. and 10 p.m. you will find certain spaces in which sit sailors in attitudes of deep thought. Some are writing. Some are chewing penholders. An instructor lieutenant-commander —known in all Ward Rooms as ' Schoolie '—or one of his schoolmasters paces between the desks with a helpful expression.

All battleships have night schools in which the ambitious can strive to rise even to commissioned rank. There is nothing to prevent a clever sea-man—if he starts young enough—reaching the Ward Room as an officer as quickly as the mid-shipman who begins at Dartmouth or a public school. Certain youths and men in every ship take the Higher Educational Test either to rise in the Navy or to educate themselves for civil life when their time is up.

How many people, I wonder, who consider themselves fairly well informed could pass the general-knowledge test which the Admiralty puts to the ordinary naval rating if he wishes to be a ruler of the King's Navy?

Here is a typical examination paper:

1. Write an essay of about 250–300 words on one of the following subjects:
    (a) Emigration;
    (b) The future possibility of English being adopted as a universal language;
    (c) The importance of the tropics.

2. Write what you know about the present-day subjects—
    Derating scheme,
    Safeguarding,
    Kellogg Pact,
    Simon Commission.

3. Choose six of the following Shakespearian characters. Name the play in which each occurs, and describe the part each takes in the play, with a quotation if possible—

Malvolio, Caliban, Iago, Ariel, Falstaff, Puck, Touchstone, Shylock, Cordelia, Jacques, Banquo.

4. Give fully your ideas about four of the following—
    (1) Is mirage entirely an optical illusion?
    (2) Can the sun's rays, shining through a water bottle, burn a table-cloth?
    (3) To what cause is the phosphorescence of the sea due?
    (4) What is meant by a gradient of 1 in 4?
    (5) Will a thick glass crack before a thin one when hot water is poured in? Does the insertion of a spoon help matters?
    (6) Is the ninth wave always the largest?

5. What is artificial silk?
    What is the nature of the following substances and what industrial uses are made of them—
    Copra, spelter, tungsten, rubber, shellac?

6. Give a short sketch of one of Charles Dickens' novels that you have read.

7. At the end of last year the B.B.C. gave programmes in commemoration of the centenary of Franz Schubert and the tercentenary of John Bunyan. Write what you know about each of these men.

8. What is the most striking difference between Norman and Gothic architecture? In what style of architecture is:
    1. The National Gallery?
    2. Westminster Abbey?
    3. Westminster Cathedral?
    What are the essential requirements of a modern large building?

9. Where were the five Test Matches (Australia versus England) played? What were the results in each? Mention any interesting details.

10. Write notes on four of the words: Carburettor, parliament, albino, quixotic, martinet, sandwich.
    And two lines on four of the persons:
    Admiral Scheer, Miss Lilian Baylis, Lord Hailsham, King Amanullah, Robert Bridges, Lord Birkenhead.

What, in the name of all that is unprintable, would the old-time sailor have said to such a paper? The time allowed the modern sailor to answer six of these ten questions is two and a half hours !

' The Admiralty, of course, do not expect a man to give perfect answers,' said an instructor-commander. ' There is a psychological end to it. We want to see how a fellow tackles such questions. It is true that a knowledge of Gothic architecture is of no use to a sailor, but by such questions we find the type of mind we want.'

VII

The most amusing object among the million and one queer gadgets on the paymaster's books in a battleship is known technically as :

PUMP, RUM, COPPER.

It is a devilish little copper pump with a bleary, jolly look about its alcoholic neck and a handle which sticks out like the peruke of a three-bottle man. This ' pump, rum, copper ' is the chief actor in a daily ceremony, which, to my mind, is the most amusing parade in the Senior Service. It is called by the descriptive name of ' Up Spirits '.

Every morning at eleven o'clock a solemn procession may be encountered making its way, via steel stairways, along narrow alleyways where the small arms are stacked in racks, bearing copper funnels, cans, measures, and, most important of all, that little rascal 'pump, rum, copper'.

The procession is headed by a member of the ship's police, and behind walks the cooper, bearing, with some dignity, the giddy copper pump. The captain of the hold is there, so also are many dignitaries, including the duty warrant officer, the sergeant of Marines, the petty officer of the day, and the chief supply petty officer—representatives of the various messes who actually draw the rum.

The procession halts above a steel manhole. The keys are produced, the manhole is opened, and, lo! there rises from the metallic cave a rich, ripe, fruity smell of rum 33 over proof!

The captain of the hold, emerging from the official ranks, descends a vertical iron ladder, and with him goes the 'pump, rum, copper', smirking and nodding his peruke in bibulous anticipation.

The issue of rum to the Navy dates, I believe, from the eighteenth century. Petty officers and warrant officers have the privilege of drawing their daily tot in its neat and powerful state; the ship's company receives it in the form of grog, which is one part rum and three parts water. Admiral Vernon, known as 'Old Grog' from his habit of walking the quarter-deck in a grogram cloak, was the first to serve out diluted rum and water to his squadron, and as a token, perhaps not of thankfulness, the men christened the drink 'grog'.

Fewer men than ever before draw their grog,

and it has, in fact, been suggested that some day the ration may cease. Those who still draw it hope that the day is far distant. Men who do not draw grog are entitled to 2*d*. a day in lieu of it.

But listen ! Down in the fruity mystery of the spirit room comes the sound of 'pump, rum, copper', as he sucks up his daily potation from a big rum cask into a portable barrel ! A rope is let down into the spirit room, the barrel is raised, and up comes 'pump, rum, copper'.

The men sent by the various messes to draw the rations come forward with their pans and their cans. They extend them towards the rum barrel, and the officers of the ritual measure out the rum to each as if it were radium. This precious fluid is then poured into the barrel, but it cannot be drawn until it has been diluted with water.

When the petty and the warrant officers' messes have drawn their neat ration, the rum barrel is padlocked, all eyes on the act ! It is then carried in state and placed under a Marine guard near the captain's quarters. Here the precious thing rests for a long, anxious, and unnecessary hour. At eleven forty-five, or thereabouts, the rum bugle sounds, and the procession reappears to carry the rum barrel forward, where its translation into grog is performed.

In a position of dignity under the bridge stands the enormous barrel with 'God Save the King' inscribed on it in six-inch letters of burnished brass. The rum cask in a battleship lives in a state of perpetual and shameless patriotism! Now comes the water, three parts to one of rum. The brew is well stirred. The pungent, ruby-red liquor is doled out until the cask has to be tilted for the last comers. The last man receives his due amount, and, most miraculously, there is not a drop of the precious stuff left over!

The patriotic cask is then set aside till the morrow. The grog has been served.

God Save the King!

Somewhere in the depths of H.M.S. *Impenetrable*, Sir Timothy Rum-pump—no longer looking like ' pump, rum, copper ', but like a dissolute Georgian squire—snoozes and nods in benevolent incapacity, well-oiled, ' shot-away ', entirely and magnificently debauched.

VIII

The drifter is a good sight. She brings the mails and the newspapers to the Fleet. During the war a touching friendship sprang up between the battleship and the Yarmouth drifter. Such ill-assorted friendships sometimes exist between Great Danes and fox-terriers of doubtful parentage.

The Yarmouth fishing smacks were invariably seen in those days nestling beneath the grey flanks of 25,000-ton battleships, engaged in light

badinage or in transactions connected with potatoes and letters from home, or both. It is a true
saying that you never know your friends until
adversity reveals them to you ; and the Fleet
found its friends, suddenly and unexpectedly, in
these wise little taxicabs of the sea, always ready
to wheel on a roaring swell and do something
useful for the big grey giants.

It seems to me a romance that the lords of
Admiralty, who are not, as a rule, touched by
sentiment or given greatly to generosity, should
have decreed that the battleships and their friends
in adversity shall not be separated in these times
of peace. So you will find that each battleship
now has attached to her for discipline, rations,
and every kind of duty, a Yarmouth drifter,
whose official capacity is that of a maid of all
work. The drifters are the Mary Anns of the
Navy.

This means, of course, that the drifter has been
smartened according to regulations. Her sloping,
villainous, piratical-looking fo'c'sle no longer
shines silver with fish scales, and she no longer
lurches into harbour like a Christmas tree hung
with mines and other flotsam of the deep. Her
brass (though this will be contradicted in high
quarters) shines (what there is of it), her woodwork is scrubbed white (or as white as possible),
and the hold, once sacred to herring and now
sacred to a young lieutenant or sub, is known with
absolute solemnity as the Ward Room.

When you see something tossing violently on the

bosom of the waters you can be sure that you have seen the drifter. You can see her most days reeling and bucketing through a head sea, with a pale-green lieutenant on her bridge, a grimy stoker petty officer coming up for air ; and, if you could see into the alleged Ward Room, you would observe an apple-green snotty rolling from side to side in the top bunk, wondering why he ever went to sea, and how even Britannia can be said to rule the waves.

The duty which endears the drifter to the Navy is that of postman. She brings the mails. It is perfectly amazing how she brings the mails but, as a matter of fact, her life would not be worth living if she failed to bring them, for the mail is the most sacred thing in the Navy. When she comes alongside with the mails a fringe of varied heads appears high up on the battleship, and a number of people look down to see a Marine standing in the reeling drifter beside two precious sacks.

At this moment the drifter is, indeed, sacred. She is a link with wives and sweethearts. Those bags contain the letters which in half an hour will spread a dead silence in Ward Room and Gun Room, and in every part of the ship. In the drifter at that moment is news of homes and children, photographs—everything that, in fact, hurts so beautifully in the Navy.

The wives of the Navy have, of course, never seen the drifter edge up with the mails. They have never seen the face of the man who stretches out his hand for a letter which is not there. He makes a bad joke, whistles, and disappears for a bit until the other fellows have read their letters, and then he wanders in and orders a pink gin. (Perhaps—to-morrow?)

The drifter can hurt like the devil.

When the Fleet makes a move the drifters attached to each ship form a little fleet on their own and 'proceed' coastwise in a manner known to them, avoiding rough weather if possible (which is not often), and following the battleships as rapidly as they can. Sometimes, in recompense for discomforts endured, the crews of drifters draw what is termed 'hard-lying money' (those who receive this are naturally known as 'hard liars'), but what degree of misery qualifies a drifter's crew to this doubtful benefit is not, it seems, laid down in naval procedure. 'Please take over from me —I'm going to be sick!' which is a request sometimes heard on the bridge, does not, as far as I can see, establish hardship. You must, it appears, have an uncomfortable bed!

On such occasions, as the drifters set out on their adventures, the fleet of Mary Anns is commanded by the senior lieutenant, who, as soon as higher authority has dropped below the skyline, becomes known officially by the self-styled title of 'A.C.D.', or admiral commanding drifters. The 'admiral' is generally a young man, who owns his first razor and has not yet broken himself of the midship-man's love of good cigarettes. It is sometimes his first real command. He amuses himself by sending out fleet orders to all the other smooth-faced young men on the bridges of his disreputable squadron :

' Admiral wishes meeting commanding officers,' he runs up on the masthead.

If the seas would make it impossible for a seal to keep an appointment with an iceberg, his trusty commanding officers may indulge in back chat, pointing out that, failing wings, the meeting is impossible, whereon the ' admiral ' may hoist the signal :

' All right. Only wanted know who's got the beer.'

In the morning, when the drifter fleet sets out on its journey, the 'admiral', instead of ordering ' single line ahead ', has been known to greet his squadron with :

' Good morning, my children ! Follow father ! '

(This has exactly the same result !)

If by chance a drifter, owing to the hazards and perils of the sea, or to the misjudgment of the young man on the bridge, grazes the stern of the one ahead, the ' admiral ' becomes immediately curious.

' Did you, or did you not, kiss that girl ? ' he signals.

' I did,' comes the answer.

' Are your intentions honourable ? ' asks the ' admiral '.

' They are not,' is the reply.

' Then kindly observe the proprieties,' orders the ' admiral '.

So the drifters, behaving exactly as Rudyard Kipling would have them behave, eventually reach their remote destination.

IX

It is guest night. Several distinguished officers from other ships are dining with us. The Marine band, stationed in the ante-room, has trickled its way through operatic selections and musical comedy, ending with the final solemnity of the National Anthem, during which we sit with lifted port-glasses.

We drift out by ones and twos. Some of us, stung to the extremes of hospitality by a guest, have perhaps been drinking champagne, and into a mind lifted richly above the common earth comes the idea that it would be good fun to rag old So-and-so or to take a jolly good whack at the posterior of a senior officer. So . . .

' Let's play Priest of the Parish ! '

' Yes ; who says Priest of the Parish ? '

A man who respects his dignity hurriedly makes up a four at cards, but, generally speaking, every one joins in.

This mysterious and painful game is played now and then when naval officers relax. It used to be played on the lower deck with a knotted rope—not a mild civilian rope, but a real rope—but in these days it is played in Ward Rooms and Gun Rooms with a knotted table napkin or a tightly rolled copy of *Country Life*. No one knows how, when, or why this game took root in the Navy. The padre tells me that it was learnt from French prisoners during the Napoleonic wars. All I know is that the whole affair smells strongly of tar and the eighteenth century, or earlier.

We sit in a circle.

The officer who is Priest of the Parish comes into the circle, carrying a table napkin tied into a fierce knot. Next to him sits an officer who is called ' Man John '.

The Priest hits the floor with his knotted clout and declares the court open. He points round the circle as each player announces the name of the cap by which he is to be known during the game. Each answers as the Priest points to him :

Mr. Blue Cap, Mr. Green Cap, Mr. Black Cap, Mr. White Cap, Mr. University Cap, Mr. Percussion Cap, Mr. Knee Cap, Mr. Night Cap . . . and so on right round the circle.

The game now consists in the interchange of a certain ritual, the slightest departure from which condemns the defaulter to one or more whacks from the knotted clout, as the Priest decrees. The clout, by the way, is termed a ' Stonachey '. Is there any one—naval man or archaeologist—who can explain the meaning of this word ? The Priest opens the game by hitting the floor with the Stonachey, saying :

' The Priest of the Parish has lost his Considering Cap. Who claims this very fine piece of

money ?   Some say this and some say that, but
I say Mr. Blue Cap. . . .'

The player who has taken the name of Blue Cap
must then immediately salute the Priest and conduct the following dialogue :

Mr. Blue Cap : ' What, me, sir ? '

Priest : ' Yes, you, sir ! '

Mr. Blue Cap : ' You lie, sir ! '

Priest : ' Who then, sir ? '

Mr. Blue Cap : ' Mr. White Cap ! '

The dialogue then moves to White Cap, and
so on round the circle.   But the slightest error in
the formula or the etiquette of the game brings
the player to disaster.   For instance, every Cap
must salute the Priest.   Not to do so is an offence.
If a player absent-mindedly salutes another player,
that also is an offence.   Every Cap in the circle
watches the Cap concerned in the dialogue in the
hope of tripping him up.   For instance, if White
Cap makes an error, Red Cap (or the first player
to notice) shouts :

' Watch White Cap ! '

The Priest then stops the ritual by hitting the
floor with the Stonachey and saying :

' Mr. White Cap watched by Mr. Red Cap.
Who claims this very fine piece of money ? '

Red Cap (or the Cap who first challenged White
Cap) then makes the following extraordinary
speech :

' I, Red Cap, claim that very fine piece of
money, likewise Mr. White Cap, who, bringing a
very fine flipper to the front, did, during the course

of this most divine ceremony, make a complete
and utter mess of his dialogue, in that he did '
—(here follows a description of White Cap's
mistake). ' I therefore beg leave to award him
with one good flip over the behind.'

If the Priest awards the ' flip ', White Cap must
immediately rise, and, turning his back on Red
Cap, bend down to receive a hearty lash from the
Stonachey, after which Red Cap returns the
Stonachey to the Priest with the remark (and a
salute) :

' All just debts and dues duly paid, most noble
lord ! '

It sounds easy. But watch and listen to a room
full of naval officers who know the game ! The
dialogue flashes round the circle. The thing is
taken at breakneck speed—so rapidly, in fact, that
it is only a question of seconds before even the
most practised player is caught out.

There are a number of technicalities which it
is rather difficult to explain. If the Priest makes
a mistake he can be watched. Then ' Man
John ' carries on for him. But during this regency
' Man John ' always refers to the Priest as ' late
Priest of the Parish ' until that ' watch ' is made
good and the Stonachey restored to the Priest.

A common cause of disaster, when the game is
played quickly, is saluting a player instead of
the Priest. Then the Watcher who catches
the defaulter demands the penalty with the
phrase :

' Likewise Mr. Green Cap, who, being one of

God's meanest creatures, did in your honour's presence dare to salute Mr. White Cap.'

When experts play the game it is not possible to avoid punishment. I have seen players pulled up for sitting with legs crossed, smoking, or behaving in a casual manner while addressing the court. Men wearing black socks in which there was visible the faintest of white lines have been punished, for 'having the audacity to appear in your worship's court wearing socks of such a nature that one might play a game of chequers thereon'.

I tried to explain this game to a woman who asked me how the Navy employs its spare time.

'What darlings they are!' she said suddenly. 'That's what I adore about the Navy! They never quite grow up, do they? Such adorable schoolboys! How perfectly sweet!'

x

When a fleet is at anchor, Sunday morning is a time of great activity. At about eleven o'clock the sea becomes dotted with boatloads of religious conviction making their way to worship. Wesleyans are seen being conveyed to the ship in which their particular padre 'hangs out'; Roman Catholics are on their way to visit the priest in another ship; smaller boatloads of 'other denominations' wind in and out of the fleet in search of their proper spiritual comfort. It is a great day for visiting.

Nearly every battleship contains some one of 'fancy religion' for whom no occupation can be found on the Sabbath.

'But the worst I ever encountered in all my experience', said a petty officer, 'was a Jew. He was the only one we had, and we were a bit vague-like about the Jewish regulations ; and he knew it ! Well, one day his sister died sudden. Up he comes to ask for fourteen days' leave. "What for ? " we asked, suspicious at once. "Why," he said, " to mourn over the body, of course, according to the Jewish faith." That didn't seem quite right to us, but we didn't want to be hard on him, so the padre wired to a rabbi or something, and, believe me, it was all flannel . . . just flannel from beginning to end.'

The padre in a battleship gets to know all the bad hats.

'Some of the worst cases', said the padre, wiping his spectacles and replacing them, 'turn out rattling good fellows. I have known real bad lots suddenly reform, fellows whose conduct sheets ran into three editions. The excuses that are dished up from time to time are most elaborate. There was Jack, who asked leave to go to Hackney to see his old mother before she died. He obtained four days' leave and returned on the eighth ! He went before the captain. He gave a vivid description of waiting for the train at

Charing Cross, then he met an " old ship " and they went to have a drink.

' " And while we was havin' a drink, sir," he said to the captain, " one of these ere Bolsheviks comes into the bar and kind of sneers at us ; and I, not wishin' to make a fracas in the King's uniform, made to go out, quiet as a lamb, when he ups and says somethin' to which I took immejet excep- tion. . . ."

' " What did he say ? " asked the captain. " I hardly likes to repeat it, sir." " Repeat it at once ! " " Well, sir, what he said was—' Down with the King ! ' " " Well ? " " I couldn't stand it, sir." " So you left ? " " No, sir, I 'it 'im ! " " And then ? " " They thought 'e was dead, sir." " So you stayed four days to find out ? " " No, sir, it would have been all right but for an interferin' cop." " Oh, I see."

' So ', said the padre, ' he went to the cells.

' Then there was the amazing Ginger. . . . When I joined a new ship some years ago I saw a notice posted up : " Volunteer wanted to be servant to the padre." Under this was written a scrawly name, and men were laughing at it. I heard such remarks as : "What, Ginger ? " " Yus, Ginger." " Then Gawd 'elp the padre ! " Ginger turned out to be an elderly, retiring, but experienced individual whose Record filled three sheets. It was an appalling record.

' But he turned out to be a model servant as long as I saved his pay and doled out a shilling a time and never enough for him to go ashore with. However, at Constantinople I smashed my watch, and I decided to send Ginger ashore with a friend to get it mended. The friend returned— but without Ginger ! The friend described how Ginger accused an Armenian watchmaker of stealing the "jools" from the watch, which, by the way,' explained the padre, ' only cost me fifteen bob, so they could not have been too precious. However, in the course of the argument the Armenian found Ginger's fist on his nose, and when the general scrap which ensued was over Ginger had vanished. The friend was sure that he would turn up. He did ! I was asleep in my bunk. Ginger entered, swaying, carrying a pail of hot water.

' " Where the devil have you been, Ginger ? " I asked.

' " I won't have you scandalized, sir," he said, spreading his fingers like a star-fish in my direction ! " I absolutely refuse to have you scandalized."

' " You're drunk," I said.

' " Less and more," he replied, " but I won't have you scandalized. They say we've the dirtiest cabin in this ship, and I won't have you scandalized."

' He then began to scrub the cabin until I kicked him out, whereupon a terrible row arose outside because some of his friends had gathered to hear the upshot of his return. It ended in a fearful fight. The strange thing is that on the following day Ginger, very meek, borrowed some

48

money, went ashore, and returned with my watch ! How he got it back is a mystery.'

Some one entered and summoned the padre.

' I must go,' he said. ' Anyhow, Ginger is now a trusted and respectable private servant.'

' By the way, padre, how's the boy who dressed up ? '

The padre laughed and went out.

This is the story of the boy who dressed up. A young sailor of seventeen was told off to clean the ship's chapel. In the corner of the chapel was a cupboard in which the padre kept his robes. One day when the ship was in harbour some visitors were being shown over her.

' This ', said a petty officer, ' is the chapel.'

He was horrified to see, leaning casually on the altar rail, a more or less religious figure which was certainly not the padre.

' And who ', asked one of the visitors, ' is this clergyman ? '

For once the composure of the Navy was shattered.

' That ', said the petty officer, hustling the visitor from the chapel, ' is the padre ! '

But he knew who it was, and the boy knew he knew ; and so it went on until the captain knew, and then, of course, the Lord High Executioner knew also !

II. THE FLEET AT SEA

THE AWNING comes down from the quarter-deck, a stir of great activity pervades the *Impenetrable* : the Fleet is going to sea.

'What are we doing now?' you ask, as a perceptible throb rises in the ship.

'Oh, mucking about!' is the reply.

You laugh to think of tons of death and destruction 'mucking about'.

'In the Navy you spend your time either mucking about or being mucked about . . . actually we are going to sea.'

And this is how a battle squadron goes to sea.

The flagship signals 'Single line ahead', and her great propellers churn the water. The early morning sun, flashing on brass-work, turns her almost white. The squadron was anchored as it came in from sea, the flagship first and the battleships in line with her, so that in leaving harbour the squadron wheels about, and the flagship, wheeling first, passes down the line. She sees the crews of each ship standing in two ranks on both sides of the fo'csle and in the waist. On the quarter-deck of each ship is the band of the Royal Marines.

The flagship moves along the line, her band playing. As she comes level with the first ship a bugler sounds the ' still '—and the crew come to attention. The flagship acknowledges the compliment similarly. Her crew also stand to attention ; and so she moves out to sea.

Bugles sound and the bo'sun's whistle is heard as ship passes ship. The junior ship pipes her crew to attention, the senior ship pipes in reply, compliment and exchange of compliment, and the grey monsters forge ahead in single line towards the white billows and the open sky.

Once at sea, the hundred activities of a battleship begin with vigour. The great noses of the 16-inch guns are seen to move blindly over the horizon as if in search of a victim. The gun turrets train easily to port or starboard. Gun crews are inside getting the turrets ready for action.

The ceremony of putting out the paravanes occupies two groups of men right forrard. The paravanes, which look like the result of a marriage between a shark and a torpedo, swim below water at a depth and a distance from the ship which draws a wide inverted V of cable on either side, to toss mines from her path.

Kate, Theresa, and big Uncle Rube, the ship's cats, come up on deck to see what is happening. Ships' cats are as different from land cats as seamen are from landsmen. They are seldom brought to sea on purpose. They generally walk aboard some dark night in harbour and take possession. Sometimes they get tired of a ship and leave her, joining that strange, much-travelled company of cats in dockyards, until they find a craft to their liking.

Uncle Rube is a person of decided habit. He is a kind of admiral among ships' cats—a creature that on fine days likes the quarter-deck and the shade of his own favourite bollard.

Great ships in line have to keep a respectful distance one from the other. The flag-ship signals every change of her speed to the next in line ; and the signal is passed on :

' One four eight revolutions,' says the officer of the watch down a brass speaking-tube, and the engine room complies instantly.

A midshipman translates this into knots and runs to the signaller on the bridge, who puts out a speed flag for the benefit of the ship behind.

In this way a battle squadron keeps its respectful stations, and landsmen on shore, seeing them at exact mathematical distance, so many cables' length one from the other, thank God for the efficiency of the Navy.

II

There is something terrifying in the thought of these steel monsters playing at war. Even although I know that the shells fired will be star shells and that the torpedoes will wear cork noses instead of T.N.T., I find myself excited and rather apprehensive. Do we really fire our big guns ? And the ship becomes taut and sensitive of the drama ahead. The calm routine of life in Cromarty Firth gives way to tense activities. The Ward Room is mysteriously empty at times when it used to be full. Only the padre is to be found. The ship has come to life.

Other well-known landmarks have disappeared. Destroyers and battle-cruisers that seemed an unalterable part of us have melted away, leaving us, a lonely squadron, steaming in a waste of water. Now and again we see a ship far off on the remote edges of the sky, a grey ship like a little grey lizard, or perhaps a destroyer flotilla crosses our path, far off, to disappear swiftly over the horizon. A seaplane, miles away, seems to fall into the waves. We look and discover the aircraft carrier, *Courageous*, just visible where sea and sky meet.

The ship throbs through the sea. There is no motion. I remember how on her trials, as I have been told, she was taken in a gale round the Scilly Isles in an unsuccessful attempt to make her ' move '. The mighty thing ploughs through the sea ; and I, standing on deck, look down and watch the green water flung over her steel plates, swirling back to form a churned wake like whipped cream. I go up on the bridge and listen to the voice of the officer of the watch as he speaks the speed down a tube. Ahead of us is the broad stern of the flagship, throbbing over the water as we are throbbing, churning the sea to whiteness. Above her funnels is a distorting flicker of heat. She alters her course and we follow faithfully in her wake, our distance from her as exact as the distance between us and our next in line.

We steam all day. Land is left far behind and the sun sets. Our wireless is busy. Signalmen run about with messages. We are going into ' action ' to-night. At some time unknown to us we will encounter ' enemy ' ships in the darkness.

Night closes in on us.

There is a sudden noise of running about and the clang of steel plates. What is it ?

' Darken ship and prepare for action ! '

That is the order. We are going into action ! What is even more startling : we are going into action in pitch darkness !

Hatches and manholes are shut down. Deadlights are closed over the scuttles. Every ray of light is hidden. In a few moments the dark ship rides a lead-grey sea in starlight.

There is nothing on sea or land more sinister, more thrilling, more nervous, than a battleship going into action at night, her heavy guns noiselessly nosing round in the dark ready for their targets, every eye, every ear strained in extreme sensitiveness.

Men descend to their stations deep down in the depths of the ship, where they can never hope to know anything of the approaching fight. All they can do is to obey the orders ticked out on dials, spoken down tubes. They can never see victory, and in war the first they can know of defeat is the sound of an explosion. From them is demanded the purest form of courage—the courage to fight an invisible foe.

I find my way over pitch-black, empty decks to the bridge. Black figures muffled in great-coats are outlined against the stars. There is a hum of subdued talk, and the voice of the officer of the watch calmly ordering new speeds down a brass tube.

'Ever seen a Christmas tree?' asks a low voice on the bridge. (It might have been 'the Pilot'.) 'The bridge of a battleship at night is rather like a Christmas tree,' says the voice, 'festooned with all the talents . . .'

So it is. The captain, with his night-glasses, the navigating officer, the officer of the watch, various others, many midshipmen in alert attitudes, and the important chief yeoman of signals standing next to the captain, his eyes strained for any message by lamp from the darkness, gaze into the night.

The great ship steams ahead: there is no sound but the hiss, hiss, hiss of the water as she cleaves her mysterious way.

Miles away the enemy fleet is steaming in a similar formation and in darkness. A queer little half-moon creeps up into the sky, turning us into a school of whales wallowing in the night. A pretty night to play at death.

'I should go to bed if I were you. This will go on for hours . . .'

I grope my way from the bridge, along the dark

waist of the ship. Crews are asleep round their gun stations. I climb down to my deck and reach my cabin.

'Wake me when the battle begins,' I say to the Marine.

'Very good, sir.'

I climb into my bunk, but I cannot sleep. The mysterious night seems to press against the steel sides of the ship. I feel uneasy and excited. I plug my ears to cut out the incidental noises of a battleship. A liner creaks and shakes. Her woodwork is always in protest. A battleship just ploughs ahead with a steady purr of propellers. But instead of the creaking of woodwork you have awful metallic interruptions. Things bang, tick and clang. The tinned air makes a rushing sound day and night. And if the engines stop you can hear the tramp of the Marine sentry pacing through the lonely watches.

III

Bang-bang-bang !

'Sir !'

'Who's that ?'

The lights are on in my cabin ! I see my servant, a khaki gas mask swinging against his chest :

'Action stations, sir.'

'What time is it ?'

'Three ack emma, sir.'

56

I fling clothes on and go out to watch a night battle. The normal stairways are shut. I climb through steel manholes like those used by sewage experts in pavements. I grope my way in pitch darkness to the deck. The moon has gone. The ship is washed in a faint green light of stars. It is cold. Ghostly groups stand silent round anti-aircraft guns. The big grey gun turrets revolve with a soft oily motion. Inside, the crews are crouched before luminous dials in the light of one ominous blue electric bulb. The thing is unreal. It is like a ghost story of the sea. I look over the starlit waters. The Fleet is steaming in pitch darkness. Ahead I can see the grey bulk of the flagship. Astern rises a thing like a grey cathedral with a thin spire : the shadow of our next in line. Away on our bows more distant shapes, low in the water, moving stealthily like a darker part of the sea—our destroyers.

There is nothing more sinister, more full of fearful potentiality, than a fleet darkened for action forging on with grim persistence into the night. What on earth would some innocent merchant ship think if she suddenly found herself among these unlit mountains ? And the guns are never still ! Their tremendous fingers move round the sky, sink, rise again, and grope blindly for something, settling at last with deliberate, cold-blooded certainty on some part of the night.

' Come along . . . things are happening ! Follow me ! '

A muffled form dives at me from the shadow of

5   57

a turret, and we go swaying doubtfully in the darkness. The ship, which seems so dead, is terribly alive. In steel turrets men are speaking down tubes, repeating orders, reading dials.

We come to darkened ladders. They lead to the bridge.

If you cannot endure suspense, keep away from the bridge of a battleship in a night action ! All the nerves of the ship are gathered there. One word from this spot, and nine tons of death can be flung at the horizon. One word, and the mammoth can slow down or leap ahead.

The few men on the bridge, and on the still higher foretop, are the only men who see anything of a naval battle. Below decks and in steel turrets over thirteen hundred men work in blind obedience. All they know of action is a voice on the telephone, a call down a speaking-tube, the flicker of an arrow over a dial. The men closed up in the steel gun turrets load their ton shells into the gigantic steel mouths—but they do not fire them ! They make an electric signal that their guns are loaded, and the guns are fired from a remote spot. The gunners do not know whether they have hit or missed ! All they know is that they must lay their guns at a certain angle, load them, and report. Below the water-line the torpedo crews stand in the same mathematical obedience.

But the bridge is a nerve centre. Messengers come and go. Men speak in jerky, unfinished sentences as they peer out through night glasses. Eerie voices come up from the depths through speaking-tubes. And all round in the darkness queer instruments which seem to have a life of their own tick monotonously. Moon-like luminous gyro-compass repeaters goggle and grin.

'Destroyer action ahead, sir.'

On the extreme edge of the sea is a glow of light and a star shell.

The muffled forms on the bridge watch intently.

'Cruisers in action on the port bow!'

The same glow and more fireworks. Then the voice of a midshipman, a youthful treble voice, very urgent and important in the darkness :

'Suspicious object on our starboard bow, sir!'

I gaze out, but can see nothing. No one pays any attention! Then the young voice again, even more urgently :

'Suspicious object on our starboard bow, sir!'

No answer. I can see nothing but the smooth motion of the sea, but I wish some one would verify the midshipman! After all, young eyes, you know! His voice again, this time tense with excitement :

'Suspicious object on our starboard bow, sir!'

The dark senior forms against the stars at last pay attention.

'Who is that idiot?' growls one.

'Suspicious object be damned!' growls another. 'It's one of our own destroyers!'

I have a vision of a midshipman in merciful darkness flying down to the nethermost depths of humiliation. Then suddenly the whole sea goes mad, and just at the moment when it goes mad there is a cry, ' *There they are !* ' and I have an impression of all our vast guns suddenly moving over to the madness and fixing themselves in rigid recognition. . . .

Star shells fired at us from the horizon parachute into the sea and die hissing in green flame. They are pitched short, and I can hear their metal bases screaming past us in the dark. All who have heard this sound before, take cover ! One comes whining over us, like a great mosquito, to knock **a** slight dent in the fo'c'sle deck.

' The Crystal Palace on firework night,' says some one on the bridge as the shells increase. But pitched-short star shells are no good. They must be fired to burn behind the target. We are safe ! The enemy does not see us. He is firing at our destroyers ! And in the glare of the shells I see these grey ships steaming in lines of white foam, sending out (in theory) torpedoes as they play their part in the game.

' By Jove, they've found us ! '

A shell whines over and blazes behind us !

Instantly the batteries of the flagship fire ; we fire next, and so on down the line ; and against the brilliant blaze of our stars we see the enemy, far away where the sea meets the sky, lying—one, two, three, four battleships—like slim, white lizards.

This is the time when, in war, our gun turrets would fling their tons of death. This is the moment when the vast ship would seem to pause in her course and rock to the side as the guns recoil. This is the time that we might put up our hands to our ears to find them bleeding.

Instead, our searchlights fall a moment into the sea and illuminate great circles of boiling waves, and then, straightening out, shoot over to the horizon and pin the enemy against the sky. He retaliates. Thin swords of light flash from the remote white lizards and, broadening, dazzle us. The whole sea is crazy with veering shafts of light. They cross and recross. They blunder over the night, discovering unexpected destroyers. The whole sea is alive. And every searchlight represents gun fire ! We are all theoretically on the brink of death ! For minutes that seem like hours we steam, dazzled and blinded, in the enemy light. Our own shafts ray out from us with sea fog in them, and it seems to us that the enemy tries to shake them off, but one little turn and we hold him ! He cannot escape ! We have him ! We had him first ! He is a mass of blood and shattered steel ! We have won. . . .

A messenger comes :

' Cease fire.'

The searchlights die one by one. The night is black as pitch. Ahead of us the flagship breaks into light.

' Undarken ship.'

We break likewise into light. The battle is over.

A destroyer lifts and tosses to starboard.

' Hi ! ' comes the hail, ' we've got your tin fish ! '

At the end of a **rope** is the shining, dripping, steel torpedo which was fired at the enemy. After a mock battle the destroyers bucket about the sea picking up ' tin fishes ' and returning them to their owners. A boat's crew is lowered and the deadly silver thing is tugged back.

' Well,' says ' Guns ' in the Ward Room, ' in action we should have let go at them at least ten minutes before we did. Cheer-ho ! '

' What really would have happened,' says some one else, ' is that we should have challenged them, both of us would have fired, missed one another, and then skedaddled out of it like the very devil— until daylight. . . . What about a cup of ship's cocoa ? '

There is a faint promise of dawn in the east, and the *Impenetrable*, vast and dark as a hill, throbs on, an escort of destroyers on her starboard bow.

IV

We are going into action by day.

In a steel compartment above the bridge the Instructor officer spikes wireless messages on a fat file, places a pair of compasses on a chart, and says casually :

' We should make contact with enemy cruisers in fifteen minutes.'

On the table before him is a remarkable sight.

It is a complete map of the invisible enemy fleet.
News of these ships has come to him from the air
and from the edges of the sky. He reminds me
of a sub-editor building up a story of a hushed-
up revolution from fragmentary dispatches which
shoot in from a dozen capitals. The wide sea,
which looks so calm, is alive with news ! The
Fleet has eyes under the water, in the air, on the
horizon and below it !

A pack of our destroyers, nosing far off like
hounds drawing a covert, has barked back information to our wireless aerial. A submarine,
unexpected as these weird fish always are, comes
dripping to the surface ten miles off to tell us
about something she has heard or seen. A
scouting aeroplane knows even more ! A cruiser
on the horizon joins in.

The Fleet, which looks so grim and silent
as it steams to battle, is really as animated and
gossipy as a woman at a tea party. And every
time a juicy piece of gossip flies through the air
for our information and necessary action, a glass
trap opens in the steel compartment, a brawny
hand shoots in bearing a message, and a Devon
voice, rich as clotted cream, says :

' Check on that last report, zur.'

' Right-o.' And the officer who has made a
map of our invisible foes gives the message a
single contemptuous glance. ' Another one joined
the reciprocal club, I suppose,'—and bends down
again over his plotting chart with the expression
of a senior wrangler.

I watch him with some reverence, remembering, rather vividly, recent criticisms of the Navy. The battleship, said one critic, is obsolete. I realize that if the battleship is obsolete so is the Navy ! A fleet is not a collection of independent units, but a closely-knit unity. Remove the battleship, and the rest of the fleet is maimed ; remove the rest of the fleet, and the battleship is futile ! You might as well say that heavy artillery is obsolete on land.

The glass trap shoots open. The hand shoots in.

'Hullo ! Enemy aircraft already. Approaching from starboard—30 degrees on the bow !'

The battle has begun !

The sea is calm. The sun is warm. (Submarines hate this weather and aeroplanes love it.) The grey mammoths are steaming in single line ahead. A cable's length from us the broad beam of our flagship rides in the white thrash of her propellers. Astern is the stately line of the battle squadron.

Every turret is manned. Crews stand ready behind steel walls. Below the water-line in the torpedo flats, other crews stand to the great steel tubes and to the cranes which lift the shining ' tin fish ' into position. Every anti-aircraft gun is ready for action. Every machine gun is trained in the direction of the foe.

We, the battleships, are the heart of the fleet ; ours the heavy guns that launch each a ton of death towards the distant sky ; and all round

64

us, sometimes just a masthead on the horizon
or a curl of regrettable smoke, are our helpers and
our guards : the destroyers screening us, the submarines, the cruisers scouting safe within the
vengeance of our armament, and somewhere,
not too far away and in a mood of maidenly
detachment, that most youthful of all our company—the big, flat, ugly floating compromise
between land and sea, the aircraft carrier. So
we steam, not as battleships, but as a battle fleet,
into action.

Look ! Our aircraft carrier is flying off her
'planes ! She steams into the wind, and they
take off—one, two, three, four, five, six—in quick
succession, circle a moment, and sweep off into
the sun. They are going to scrap with enemy
aircraft.

But where are these enemy 'planes ? The sun
shines on our starboard bow. Our eyes ache
with gazing at the sun. Some one hands me a
smoked glass, and I look up into the glare for
those who are coming to bomb and torpedo us.

' Destroyer action ahead ! ' says some one on
the bridge in a calm, conversational voice.
Through glasses I see, far off where sea and sky
meet, our pack of hounds scattering here, there
and everywhere, from a hive of enraged hornets.
The aeroplanes swarm over them, dive down at
them, and skim their mastheads. The pattern
of their attack changes as our fighter 'planes
jump into them. Two and two they wheel and
loop and dip, pursuer and pursued, high above

the scattered flotilla. Suddenly a black hood falls over the scene. The destroyers have put up a smoke screen. The thing lies on the waves like a range of black mountains ; and there is no more to see.

One of the surprising things to me is the ease and secrecy with which aeroplanes can come out of the sun on to their target. There is a moment when the sky is seemingly clear. The next moment there is a roar of engines and the shadows of attacking 'planes. But naval eyes are keener. The hornets are upon us, but the hornets are seen.

Our guns nose blindly round, and then settle on them with grim and frightful intelligence. But over us, astern of us, ahead of us, on port and starboard, has broken the thing that Jutland never knew—seamen are fighting airmen.

It is a thrilling, maddening combat. One is torn between a desire to stand these mad pilots a drink and let off a gun at them just to teach them a lesson ! One little flycatcher throttles back his engine and dives at our foretop as a moth dives at a candle. He sprays us with machine-gun fire. His engine roars again just as he seems about to trip up in our wireless. He does it again ! The roar of him fills the ship. One of our fighters makes a dive for him, and off they go into the sky.

On our starboard and port bows the torpedo 'planes are busy. They dive as if to death, but when within twenty feet of the sea a shining torpedo falls from them and crashes down into

66

the water in a plume of flung spray. When torpedoes are out a fleet side-steps. All rules are broken. No one thinks of the admiral. It is get out or go under.

So, as these audacious, devilish hornets lay their bright eggs in the sea the greatest battleships in the world stampede in an effort to steer clear of the beautiful, pale-green lines that are drawn steadily towards them along the surface of the water. A torpedo is a determined fish. It does not rush at you. It swims at an even but rather inevitable pace, and you can see it coming.

The aeroplanes appear. They do their fantastic worst. They disappear. The great ships swing into line again. The admiral resumes control of formation, and a signal rating appears with a message (which from his general expression might read : ' Arrived safely, love from auntie ') containing the information that in five minutes the main battle fleets will be flinging tons of steel at one another over a wide space of sea.

The real battle is beginning.

In the Ward Room, after the war, men relax, wondering humorously whose next-of-kin would have been affected had this been the real thing !

' Surely the air attack would have finished us ? ' I ask.

' Not likely. Suppose we could have let off our " Archies " ? '

' But those torpedoes ? '

' Don't exaggerate torpedoes, old son. You've

67

been contaminated by critics. Take it from me, the Navy knows what to expect from the air. You've seen an air attack under ideal conditions. There are others.'

Senior officers wade into the debate. With extreme caution and great fairness the danger of attack by air is discussed. It is agreed that the air arm is, at the moment, only an auxiliary arm. The aeroplane is, to a battleship, only a submarine operating above the waves. The day may come, however . . .

That is the day that seems foreshadowed by a swarm of aeroplanes above the fleet : a day of mighty flying craft, Jules Verne cruisers perhaps, something different and more formidable than any aeroplane known to us. But that day is not yet. The aeroplane to-day is only the youngest arm of that much mightier weapon, the battle fleet. It is also, perhaps, the most promising.

HIS BODY TO THE DEEP

I

THE ENGINEER-COMMANDER sat on the verandah of the Miramar Hotel drinking a whisky and soda. On the floor beside him was a bunch of flowers : big white and blue Spanish flowers like convolvuli, rather exotic, and powdered with the dust of the roads.

'Hullo ! Where's the wedding ? ' asked a friend, nodding at the flowers.

'It's Stoker Davis,' replied the engineer-commander, finishing his drink. 'Dead.'

'Bad luck . . . What are you drinking ? '

'Oh, Scotch.'

From the verandah of the Miramar Hotel you can see the blue-green waters of Pollenza Bay lying cupped between harsh, volcanic hills. The white, flat-roofed houses sprawl, with the careless grace of a wild animal, in a half-moon at the edge of the sea. The bay is so clear that you can look down to weedy forests standing still as a scene in a glass water-globe. The light, striking down to white sand, turns the water to a green so pale and brilliant that you are surprised, when you cup a handful, to find it colourless. On this sand lie brown and iridescent shells, the shape of mussels, some of them the height of a man.

The British Fleet lends to Pollenza Bay an ominous air of invasion. It is so British and the

69

hills are so alien, rising in day-long sunlight, sharp-cut against a blue sky. The battleships, which look slate-grey in the North Sea, seem almost white in Mediterranean sunlight. They lie in long lines, stretching to the open sea ; and the Majorcans never tire of standing in their rocky vineyards, watching with their dark Moorish eyes the picket-boats cutting white lines in green water.

'Well, chin-chin,' said the engineer-commander. 'I must catch the five o'clock boat.'

He picked up his armful of flowers.

'Pretty poor stuff, but the best I could get.'

He walked to the little stone jetty where two seamen in the battleship's motor-launch stood jabbing the rough stones of the pier with boat-hooks, the launch rising and falling on the swell, her engine just ticking over. They knew that he had gone ashore to get flowers for to-morrow's funeral. Who was Stoker Davis ? They had been speculating about their dead shipmate. Was he the Rugger player ; or was he the fellow with a deep scar on his face ?

Stoker Davis was a swarthy Welshman from Cardiff. Beneath the rich, dark hair of his chest the name Annie was faintly tattooed in blue ink. On his right forearm was an anchor in red and blue, accompanied by such a riot of redundant cables that it looked like the work of an artist who, carried away by his enthusiasm, did

not know when to stop ; on his left arm sat a
mermaid with a mirror.

My first impression of Stoker Davis was of two
dark Iberian eyes that followed me round the sick
bay like an animal watching from a cave. I
had been developing photographs in the surgeon-
commander's dark-room and was employing my
time talking to the ship's invalids while the films
were fixing. Stoker Davis chilled me. Something told me that he was going to die. The
neat, slung bed in which he lay looked like his
shroud, and I was filled with pity and a horrible
interest. He was setting off on this terrible
adventure of dying. He could move his eyes and
talk to me and in a few days, perhaps, he would
be lying sewn up in his hammock at the bottom
of this foreign sea, rolling to the under-water
swells while strange coloured fish just touched
him with their mouths and flashed away.

I sat down beside him. We talked about
Cardiff and Barry and the long road that goes
up the valley to Pontypridd. He had strained
himself inside. They had X-rayed him twice.
He found it impossible to move, and he had
suffered a bad haemorrhage. Could I do anything for him ? Even while I asked, I felt the
futility of it because nothing mattered to him
now. But, on the edge of death as he was, he
asked me if I could find him a detective story.
I went to the ship's store and picked out three
shockers in yellow jackets. I took three because,
afraid and startled by the thing I knew, I wished

to create the illusion that he might live long enough to read them. When I got back he was lying, unconsciously pleating the sheets with his great, slow fingers, his dark eyes turned to the scuttle which framed a vivid circular picture of khaki hills in the warm hush of a Mediterranean afternoon. Some one had placed a cup of custard beside him, but he had only eaten one spoonful.

Subconsciously, I think, he knew that he no longer belonged to the Navy, and he liked me to sit beside him because I was a civilian and had nothing to do with the ship. Even the padre would not have been quite the same. And I knew Cardiff.

When I was going he fixed me with his frightening eyes, into which all his vitality was gathered, and told me that if only they would stop working the main derrick he thought he might sleep for a little. He lifted one finger :

' Listen,' he said.

And I heard above us the sound of the main derrick, stopping, starting, stopping, starting :

' Good God, why didn't you tell some one ? '

He looked at me and said nothing. It was to him incomprehensible, perhaps, that the main derrick might be stopped for him.

' I'll see the surgeon-commander at once.'

He thanked me with a slow movement of his hand.

The ship's surgeon was standing in his laboratory gazing at a pink fluid in a glass phial. I told him about the derrick.

72

'I'll have it stopped at once,' he said. 'Why didn't the man tell me?'

'Oh, I don't know. I suppose he didn't like to. By the way, you know, of course, that he's going to die?'

'Why do you say that?'

'I just feel it. There's something grey and powdery about him. You know . . .'

The surgeon-commander went into the sick bay, and I watched him reading the temperature chart which the orderly held out to him. He bent down and spoke to Stoker Davis.

'I'm worried about him,' he said when we came back. 'Two days ago I thought he'd pull through. I can't take him to sea next week, so I've arranged for him to go to the hospital ship to-night. He'll be more comfortable there. . . . He's pretty bad.'

I went ashore that afternoon and walked for miles over the hills. I heard a man and a girl singing in a vineyard. It was one of those frank courting songs which the peasants sing in southern countries. The man probably praised her hips and her breasts and paused for her to sing back to him. And when they were not singing I could hear the click of their rakes in the hot, stony soil. I tried hard to forget Stoker Davis, but he haunted me. Violent, quick death at Jutland would not have been so very dreadful: it was this slipping quietly away in alien sun-

6

light, so far from a long road in South Wales, that was so pitiful. If only a woman could have looked after him. Perhaps Annie, whose name was buried in the hair of his chest, might have comforted him. How strange that the thought of one man's death, in a ship made for the sole purpose of killing men, should seem so tragic !

As I walked over the hills I almost forgot him in thoughts of the Balearic singers, and in the joyful smell of the rosemary that lay like incense in the hot afternoon. There was a little cove whose sand was so white that it hurt the eyes, and the water that filled it was so green that I could see stones lying far out in it. I lay there and thought that I could drink a flask of the red Spanish wine that Francesca brings up from some cool depth of the Miramar Hotel ; Francesca with her ugly felt slippers and her woollen stockings and her exquisite oval face, like carved ivory, her soot-black hair parted evenly and so sleekly that it looked like black enamel. I once saw a black panther behave like a cat with a visitor at the Zoo. Francesca was like that. It was amusing to watch her countering the pleasantries of some fair-haired Englishman, he so pink and obvious, she so dark and incalculable.

I came down out of the hills as the sun was setting. The ship's boat was waiting at the jetty. We pushed off with our cargo of officers in flannels and tweed coats, and half-way across the bay we heard the bugles of 'Sunset' and saw the White Ensigns falling from the masts of the

Fleet. The boat rocked as we shut off the engine and stood to attention. In a little while we exploded beneath the grey cliff of the battleship.

That night after dinner the surgeon-commander said to me :

'That fellow—I'm afraid he's a goner.'

'Stoker Davis ?'

'Yes. He died before we could transfer him to the hospital ship.'

Our signal lamps winked at the flagship through the lovely southern night :

'Request permission,' they said, 'to bury Stoker Davis.'

After an interval, the lamps of the flagship responded. She replied to us like a nicely brought up matron from Tooting :

'Granted.'

That was her economic reply. And I walked the quarter-deck under the bright stars, knowing the strange feeling of living in a battleship with a dead man. I also wondered who Annie was, and if she still cared.

II

The superstition of sailors has always concerned itself with the presence of a corpse aboard ship. In the old days men must have lived for a little time in dreadful contact with the dead body of their shipmate, and his empty bunk, his belongings, his knife and fork, his boots must

have served as a continual reminder of the fate
that overtakes us on sea or land. But in a modern
battleship with its crew of over a thousand men,
some of whom do not know each other even by
sight, it might be thought that the death of one
man would pass unnoticed.

Death is the heaviest cargo a ship can carry.
It weighs on the spirit and, go where you will,
you cannot escape from it. Stoker Davis when
alive had been one of the least important members of the community, dead he pervaded the
ship. No one talked about him, but every one
was conscious of him.

Two Marines stood outside the ship's chapel
with bowed heads above reversed arms. Every
time a man climbed from one flat to another,
every time he ran out of the sunlight and descended the ladders to the waist of the ship, he
saw these two silent men in an attitude of mourn-
ing. His step in nailed boots softened instinctively on the steel rungs of the ladder. And
inside the chapel lay Stoker Davis sewn in his
hammock like a Theban king. The sight of
him shocked me. He looked like a contortionist
who might suddenly break his shackles and leap
out of his sack. My eye noted the rough stitch-
ing. It was a ghastly moment when his friends
placed a shell at his feet and threaded their bod-
kins with twine. I had the fearful idea that he
was not dead. Only a few hours ago was he not
looking at me with big, dark eyes and whispering
about the main derrick and the Rhondda Valley?

The last sight at night, as I went to my cabin, was the guard with bowed heads, and the first sight in the greyness of the morning were those two official mourners bent stiffly, their elbows at right angles, their chins above the butts of their rifles. The only armed sentries in the battleship were posted for the captain and for Stoker Davis. The dead man became an important, uncomfortable presence. He had ceased to obey. Yet he still belonged to us ; and in a most terrifying way we associated some part of ourselves with him. I longed for the time of his funeral so that the heaviness of Death might be lifted from the ship ; but at the same time I feared it, almost as though a piece of myself were going overboard with him to fight and struggle for breath in the sea.

'I hate funerals,' said an officer in the Ward Room.

'I ask nothing better than to be buried at sea,' said another. 'I have spent all my life at sea. And—it's clean. . . .'

Just before sunset the battleship weighed anchor and put out to sea. We steamed between the grey lines of our companion ships towards that bluer line at the bay's mouth where the Mediterranean lay smooth to the horizon and Africa. It was a lovely evening with a brown heat-mist on the edge of the sky and a few stars already out.

The officers gathered in the Ward Room wearing frock-coats, epaulettes and swords. We could hear the ship's company mustering above. Gradually the sound of our turbines altered. We were no longer steaming ahead.

I stood on one of the gun turrets near the quarter-deck and saw that we rode silently almost out of sight of land. The crew paraded as if for church. On the starboard side of the quarter-deck the platform of the accommodation-ladder had been shipped. But no steps led down from it. The perforated board stretched out into emptiness; and far below it was the sea.

' Ship's company—Attention ! '

And the crew stiffened as Stoker Davis was carried to the quarter-deck. Stokers bore him on a stretcher over which was draped a Union Jack. But the flag could not hide him. The cold evening wind that gets up at sunset nipped and pulled at the corners of the flag, and we saw the coarse canvas and the big stitches. The padre in his surplice followed, reading from an open book, and behind walked stokers holding, pitifully and shamefacedly, a wooden cross made in the carpenters' shop on which were draped faded Spanish flowers, with the road's dust in them. The body was placed with clumsy tenderness on the gang-plank, and there was no sound but the voice of the padre lifted in the open air.

The stokers stood with bent heads round the plank, big men like Davis, with big red necks, the wind moving their sailor collars. And the terrible thing about them was this : they had been crying. They looked at the Union Jack with a kind of stricken intensity, and now and then a hard knuckle would creep up to a cheek. They alone in the ship had known Stoker Davis as a man.

I looked at the flag and at the shape beneath it, longing for, and fearing, the final moment. It was a strange scene. The grey ship with its mighty guns. The men who are trained to kill. And on each face gravity or grief. . . .

The padre made a sign to the men near him and they bent quickly, fumbling with the gang-plank. It slowly tilted. The tilt became sharper. But nothing happened. Then the form of Stoker Davis in his hammock moved away from the tied flag and lay in the pale glow of sunset, poised above the sea. His body refused to fall from the plank as if he were desperately trying to remain with us. Every time the plank was more steeply tilted it seemed like a cruelty to him, as if we were banishing him. Suddenly, with a scraping sound, he dropped into the air. The heavy weight at his feet pulled him towards the sea, and as he fell the long way from deck to water his shoulders hunched as if he were alive, as if he were struggling to get out. He hit the water violently, sending up a quick white spray ; then he see-sawed a moment in a green wave and disappeared.

There was a little splash. Far below us a cross covered with half-dead flowers tilted itself

79

in the sea. It remained a moment over the place where Stoker Davis had fallen, but then waves washed it against the steel plates of the ship, swung it about and carried it astern like a wreck. We saw it bobbing in the track of the sun, and in its inability to remain above the grave we knew that this man's body was for ever lost.

Rifles were fired at the sky and bugles played the 'Last Post'. And for some minutes the grey ship drifted on the sea, waiting until Stoker Davis had gone down into his grave before the propellers would cut the water.

We steamed back by starlight into the shelter of the hills. I leant over the rail with the chilling feeling that Stoker Davis was calling to us from the darkness of the open sea. He was so alone, this man from Cardiff, in a waste of foreign waters, moving in the ebb and flow of dark currents with a woman's name written on his flesh.

Somewhere along the rocky shores of Pollenza Bay a wooden cross would be washed up and brown children would seize it, laughing, and make toys of it.

ABOUT WOMEN

THE WIFE

THE ORDINARY wife lives in an ordinary home, sometimes with an extraordinary husband, who, in his heart of hearts, thinks she has an easy time. Can she not stay at home when he is forced unwillingly to meet the rain of a summer morning in perpetual pursuit of money? Compared with his complicated life her little problems are purely childish.

If he is one of those 'homey' men who love to potter and snoop about the house like an amateur plumber, he secretly envies her. How happy he would be if he could stay at home all day and just muddle around delightfully. If he is a sterner type he likes to think of the ease and comfort which his strenuous efforts have brought to the woman of, I was going to say, his choice.

In accordance with the romantic English custom she is penniless, and therefore at his mercy. If he turns out a bad lot she is tied to him by pride, necessity, or children. Sometimes he is amused to observe her working up prettily to a request for money. Instead of saying, 'You need a new costume and I would like you to have it,' he waits for her to sit on the arm of his chair and wheedle round him:

'I wonder if you could let me have a cheque. . . .'

'What for?'

'I haven't had anything new for ages.'

'But that thing you've got on is beautiful! Surely you don't need a new one yet!'

'Surely you don't need a new one yet!' How can he know that she has fallen in love with a dress in a shop-window as fiercely as a boy with a steam engine; that she hardly dares to look in the window in case some other woman has taken that dress.

It seldom occurs to him, unless he is an unusual type, that it is humiliating for her to beg; he does not attempt to save her from it; in fact, he rather likes it; it makes him feel generous and powerful.

In the sharp, temperamental clashes, for which small houses are designed, he sometimes thinks that he has made a bad bargain—that all men make bad bargains. Surely, he thinks, some wives try to become proficient at their jobs. It is true that her early life was devoted to the arts and not to the stern practicalities of an unpaid profession. (But surely not unpaid? Is he not the reward?) She was taught to play the piano badly and to sing sickly ballads and to paint messy water-colours, achievements which served their purpose and invested her in those romantic days with a spurious halo of cleverness.

He thinks in dyspeptic moments, as the shoulders of sheep and the ribs of bulls follow one another across his table in dull and unimaginative procession, that were he a wife he would have set himself to learn the profession of housekeeping

from A to Z. He would have become the best
housekeeper on earth.

He would have studied cookery and have invented dishes. He would have invented all kinds
of things. He would have surrounded himself
with proficient and obedient servants (' Of course,
they can be found ! ') who would leap respectfully
to his orders instead of pottering round in slipshod
revolt.

After all, what is there to manage in a small
house ?

She, having long ago descended from the hills
of romance into the deeper but less exciting valleys
of affection, finds herself surrounded, swamped,
smothered, and obsessed by the trivial. At the
back of her mind is the mournful reflection that
had she not been so surrounded, swamped,
smothered, and obsessed she might have been
vaguely brilliant at—what ? That is not clear.

In her moments of dyspepsia she feels shut up
in a box. There is no escape. The wide, thrilling
world goes on outside and she is cooped up with
an unwilling girl, tied to perpetual problems
concerning the buying of minute quantities of
milk, bread, meat, and vegetables.

Her life is a stupid routine of ordering dust to
be removed from rooms designed to hold as much
dust as possible ; of ordering the minute portions
of food to be cooked ; of seeing that the plates
which contained the food are washed up ; distress-
ing trivialities which go on three times a day year
after year. She is the slave of cleanliness, cookery,

and monotony. She knows that she is an amateur, but she does her best with shocking bad material and little money ; she knows that she is no organizer ; but she does not realize that she is one of millions of similar amateurs who support, instead of combining to abolish, the stupid tyranny of the kitchen. Some day a wife will press a button and food will shoot in from a communal kitchen ; she will press another and the remnants of the feast will disappear.

It is only the capacity which women have for suffering in silence and their instinctive inability to combine which have preserved the stupidities of the kitchen.

She can sense every mood of her husband. She knows at once when he is laboriously carrying a secret ; when he is clumsily trying to hide anything. He, on the other hand, is blind to those occasions when, watching him sitting so placidly after his exciting day, she longs to utter a loud scream and hit his bald head with the nearest metal implement. She wishes at times that he was less fond of his home. He is becoming part of the unadventurous routine. Is there no excitement in life ; no unexpectedness ? It is also the anniversary of their wedding. He has forgotten. She says to him hopefully :

'George, what day is it to-day ? '

'Thursday,' he replies promptly, looking over the evening paper.

'Hullo,' he adds, 'what's up ? '

'Don't speak to me ! ' she cries, and bursts into

tears; which pains and horrifies him. An entirely comfortable world has been suddenly shattered for no reason whatsoever! In a moment of accidental inspiration he suggests a dinner and a theatre. In the taxicab on the way back he thinks she looks rather brilliant. He kisses her, feeling slightly foolish. She responds with great enthusiasm. She is like something escaped. Later, when screwing his neck round to battle with his starched collar, he says:

'We must . . . damn this stud . . . go out a bit more . . . oh, confound the thing!'

'Do you love me?' she asks with alarming earnestness.

'You know I do. Good Lord—what's the matter now?'

'Oh, nothing, only I'm so—I can't help it— happy!'

(Women, so think these excellent husbands, are really *most extraordinary*.)

THE WOMAN NOBODY KNOWS

PEOPLE WHO meet her on the stairs of the Bloomsbury Private Hotel say that you can see she is a lady. They mean that you can see she has descended the social scale from unknown altitudes. No one knows her because no one has ever had the courage to penetrate that high-nosed reserve by which she is surrounded.

It almost seems at times that she breathes her own private supply of air. No visitors climb the stairs to her little room near the roof from one year's end to the other; no letters come for her except during the reckless generosity of Christmas-time.

She is linked to the outside world by a brace of pheasants, which arrive suddenly and mysteriously in the autumn; and it is characteristic of her isolation that she rejects them—not liking pheasant—and presents the birds to the management with a bountiful gesture which invests them with a certain aristocracy. Every one feels that the birds have been blown to death by, at least, a duke.

Her slightest action is important, such as the raising of her lorgnette at dinner in order to observe the carcass of a new commercial traveller, a scrutiny which she performs with upper-class directness of motive. No one could imagine that she was examining the depressing picture, ' Highland Cattle,' under which he uneasily sits ; she is obviously looking at him, not critically or contemptuously, but just looking.

She feeds the immortal cats in the square with the air of a *grande dame* distributing alms to the tenantry. Romantic girl undergraduates staying in the hotel before they find bed-sitting-rooms in Gower Street, watch her covertly as she sits apart at her private table crumbling bread in her long yellow fingers on which the rings are loose, thinking that such were the women who calmly and disdainfully went to the guillotine as if towards a reception at the Tuileries.

She is, possibly, sixty.

It is apparent to the least practised student of human beings that she lives apart in a little paradise, or perhaps drawing-room, of memory. She is as self-contained in her own atmosphere as a goldfish in its bowl.

In the summer, when the private hotel is enlivened by Americans, she causes an uneasy hush as she enters the dining-room ; and when she has gone a voice whispers : ' Guess that old dame lines up with English history.' Some one always opens the door for her as she retires.

She is the widow of Albert Cheesepairer, merchant, of White Lodge, Sydenham, and the daughter of Sir John Knife, M.P., Master of the Worshipful Company of Cutlers of the City of London, sometime merchant of London Wall. She was born the year Queen Victoria laid the

7   89

Albert Hall foundation-stone—the same year that
Canada was proclaimed a Dominion. She was
married to Albert in the year of the good Queen's
jubilee, in the face of family opposition, and
with the full force of a passionate nature. Her
hair was originally red.

White Lodge, Sydenham, in which the brief
drama of her life was played, had stabling for six
horses, hot-houses, underground quarters for sub-
missive menials, and a marvellous view over
London to St. Paul's. It meant something in
Victorian society. There was a butler, a wine-
cellar, a pretence at art—crystoleum painting,
embroidery, Tennyson, Browning. This society
reacted quickly to Mayfair, popping in and out
of Whitby jet in response to the many family
sorrows which an unjust fate visited on the head
of royalty.

She cut rather a dash in Sydenham—the
daughter of Sir John Knife, M.P.—and people
were always glad to be invited to one of those
cumbersome dinner-parties, Georgian in general
design, over which she presided, red-haired, white-
shouldered. She never looked more lovely than
just before the port, when, gathering the assembled
women with a comprehensive smile, she rose and
led the way to the drawing-room with a crisp
sound of silk petticoats.

In marrying Albert she was said to have thrown
herself away, one of the most delicious sensations
known to woman. She was fortunate in having
enough money to be able to quarrel with every

member of her family, a truly delightful situation
for a spirited wife.

She believed Albert to be a really rich man until
the day they brought him home on a stretcher
with a large and efficient hole in his forehead.
That was in the year of the big City smashes when,
one by one, the 'Sale by Auction' boards
appeared in many large and assured-looking front
gardens in the outer suburbs.

Even this did not prove to her that her family
were in the right. Shakespeare was not thinking
of women when he said that the 'evil that men
do lives after them'. One of the humbling facts
of life is the angelic loyalty which women feel for
the most worthless men.

She gathered together the haphazard objects
which people save from a fire—carriage clocks,
photographs, scent-bottles, engraved toilet sets,
an odd Hepplewhite chair—and became submerged in a small red house in a row of small red
houses. The family rallied round, extending a
little timely assistance, but she shook her still
almost red head and declined it without
thanks.

Gradually she drew nearer to that bed-sitting-
room in a private hotel which waits for all 'gentle-
women in reduced circumstances'.

People wonder who and what she is, as they pass
her dignified, resigned figure on the stairs. There
are hundreds of women like her in London ; and
no one ever knows what is behind that grim
locked-up air of theirs. They think that they are

'stuck up'; or they think that they have 'come down in the world'.

They would be surprised, humbled perhaps, if they could see inside those pitiable rooms in Bloomsbury where these women spend the rest of a life which no longer seems very important.

The commercial traveller who suffers from Mrs. Cheesepairer's scrutiny would be surprised to know that she looked at him so closely, not because his coat was a bad cut, not because his tie was a bit noisy, but because there was something about him in that light, something just for a second, that reminded her of Albert when he was young, ambitious, and undeniable.

That air of stern reserve is the armour that a proud spirit wears against the world which has hurt it. It melts utterly under the Bloomsbury roof in the little room where the Woman Whom Nobody Knows sits alone through long hours remembering things which once were real.

Then the dinner-bell sounds. She takes up the photograph of the man who flung her so violently at Fate, and smiles. Then, becoming at once the unapproachable old lady whom nobody knows, she walks stiffly to her secluded table and tomato soup.

THE WOMAN OF AFFAIRS

THIRTY YEARS ago the 'Woman of Affairs'
was quite a different person. . . .

The girl, who was perhaps twenty-six, entered
the grill-room and sat at a table. She wore a
tailor-made costume of light grey flannel, and her
neck, which was long and white, rose from the
golden-brown gloss of the stone marten. Her
hat, small and black, was transfixed by a small
diamanté brooch.

There are still a few restaurants in the City of
London which, by tradition, are sacred to men.
They are perhaps the last strongholds of the male.
Vast quantities of fillet steak are consumed here
in an atmosphere of cigars and finance. Port
is not unknown.

Men gather round a table and prod the raw
meat before the chef tosses it on the silver grill.
They are fond of pancakes and rum omelettes,
but, generally speaking, they prefer gorgonzola.

The grill is really the annexe to a thousand
offices. Not one of the men, who is to be seen
there day after day throughout the year, would
dream of taking his wife or daughter there. The
grill-room is too closely connected with business.
Big deals have been 'put over' at its tables ; it
has nothing to do with the softer side of life.

A hundred men, therefore, regarded the stray
girl with some interest. Those sitting with their

backs to her judged their time and stole a glance at her ; those facing her regarded her, not with the alert French eye to possibilities or with the frank inquisitiveness of the Italian, but with an almost brotherly resentment. You could hear them thinking :

' You really ought to know better than to come blundering in here ! I wonder who you are ! '

The girl, apparently unconscious of herself, summoned the waiter with one small uplifted finger :

SPECIAL THIS DAY.
ROAST PORK AND APPLE SAUCE.

' I'll have some roast pork, potatoes, and French beans.'

' Anything to drink ? '

' A glass of water.'

She looked at her watch with a quick, confident, out-and-in movement of her left wrist. The three men sitting at her table admired her self-possession. None of them would have behaved so well in a roomful of women.

Before they brought the pork she turned the empty chair next to her against the table. She had reserved it for—a man or a woman ? What man would have brought a pretty girl of twenty-six to lunch in this place under the eyes of all his business associates ?

' So sorry I'm late.'

A big, hard-faced man of about fifty came in, shook hands with her, and sat down in the reserved seat.

94

The men at her table thought : ' He can't be her father, or he wouldn't have shaken hands with her ! Must be business ! '

They soon heard.

' The estimates are all wrong ', said the girl, composing a mouthful of pork on her fork, ' and I wouldn't touch them with a barge pole.'

The man looked at her with genuine interest and respect.

' I wondered what you'd think of them,' he said.

' I advise you to have nothing to do with them. If you take my advice you'll also have nothing to do with X. Cut him out.'

' But look here, I have no reason to——— '

' I know what you're going to say. You are going to tell me that the 1926 percentages were higher by one and a third.'

' I was, as a matter of fact.'

' But you forget the biggest factor of all. Look here . . . '

The girl leaned slightly towards him and made her points one by one emphatically. The man listened, eating, nodding his head, more than once turning to look at her with unconcealed admiration. Hers was the dominating brain. It was obvious that she knew what she was talking about. It was rather amusing to hear her say to the big hard-faced man of fifty ' Your big danger is this ', or ' For goodness' sake keep clear of that ! ' or ' Do look six months ahead ! '

You can tell when a man is humouring a

woman, when he is letting her talk her head off; you can tell when a woman is reeling off nonsense. This girl was talking hard commerce, and the man was glad to take her opinion.

She finished the pork :

' I'd like a strawberry ice,' she said.

That ice humanized her. It proved that she was not all chartered accountant. A most reassuring ice !

They finished. She stood up, prettily dusted off crumbs which clung to the light grey flannel, tucked her umbrella under her arm and went out.

' By Jove, pretty hot stuff that ! ' said one of the men at the table. ' She knew what she was talking about.'

' Yes ; the old boy took it all lying down. . . . Waiter, bill, please. . . .'

What would dear grandmother have thought about it ?

IN THE CITY

SHE KNOWS that the business has something to do with the selling of bath tubs to an unwashed universe—bath tubs in almost impolite quantities—but beyond that she has never inquired ; neither does she care. Just as the private soldier fails to interest himself in the finer points of strategy, so she in her modest capacity remains disinterested and incurious, coming promptly at 9 a.m. and leaving promptly at 5 p.m.

She finds herself on arrival in a friendly pen of similar femininity. She hangs her small hat on a peg among other small hats. She gazes critically at herself in a mirror, almost as though she had never before seen herself. She shakes her hair free with a sudden violent movement of the head, and turns to face the events of her unvarying day.

' Hullo, darling ! I've had my hair waved. It feels awful ! Has old Grouch rung yet ? '

' Have you heard, dear ? Milly's engaged ! '

' You don't say ! Who to ? '

' That boy with the piggy eye-lashes we met at the Cinderella last year. You know—Tom. Do you think she's pretty ? '

' Yes ; in a way.'

' So do I—in a way.'

Beyond, and all round them, the vague mysteri-

97

ousness of providing the earth with bath tubs goes
on with accustomed daily vigour, and a coming
and going of eager, preoccupied men and earnest
women secretaries, a banging of doors, a ringing
of bells and loud inner ' hallos ' on the telephone.
The vivid, much-alive girls in their neat pen—
deal knee-desks, open-work iron and leather seats,
uncovered typewriters—are concerned with a
million private affairs of more vital interest to
them than the business which brings them
together. Their interest in the firm is concerned only with personalities. ' Old Grouch '
is a pig. Mr. Hicks is a darling. Miss Johnson
is a sneak. . . .

They are the pretty butterflies of Commerce.

She has ' no need to do anything '. She could,
if she liked, stay at home and ' help mother ' ;
but she does not like. She prefers the social
excitement of the office, the train journey, the
lunch hour at the tea-shop, the confessions, the
confidences, the afternoon tea with its one sweet
biscuit ; and the unreal stimulation in the air
caused by dozens of more interested persons
foisting ridiculous bath tubs on a needy world.
She has—and this is important—two legs. These
legs deserve and demand a regular supply of silk
stockings. Her head must have the right kind
of hat ; her pretty little figure pays well for the
dressing.

You must not confuse her with the typist
secretary or with the Typist Intellectual, who are
quite different people, or with the Typist of

Necessity, that gallant girl who helps to support a family.

She is just a girl who lends the City the charm of her youth and gives it the benefit of her capricious spelling for a few weekly pounds, which she spends on the beautification of her rather lovely self. She is essentially temporary. Even in her most concentrated moments she has an air of a stray sunbeam. Security of tenure, which is the grim ghost behind so many workers, does not haunt her. If she got 'the sack' she would just flutter off to another place with the same kind of peg for a hat, the same conversations, the same tea-shop, the same biscuits in the afternoon. . . .

Some day another girl will say breathlessly :
' Have you heard the news ? Hilda's married ! '
So she will have fluttered off over deeper waters.

But—b-r-r-r-r-ing !

Old Grouch's bell !

' Miss Jones, take this down, please. . . .'

Old Grouch looks over his tall winged collar like a horse over a gate. He clears his throat and begins importantly :

' Dear Sir.'

She sits meekly, notebook open on her knee, pencil poised. He can see only the upper, unexpressive portion of her ; the lower, disturbingly expressive portion is hidden by his desk. She has a way of crooking her left ankle round the leg of the chair. She is distinctly pretty.

' " In reply to yours of the sixteenth ult."—no ; cross that out ! Say : " With reference to yours of the sixteenth ult., I regret to inform you that it is not advisable to grant—" What have you got ? Read it out ! Not advisable to grant. . . . Cross that out ! Say : " We do not think it advisable—no, expedient—to grant special discount to Messrs. Humble, Crumble, and Bumble. I am informed—no ; I understand . . ." '

She eventually escapes. Her bell rings. Mr. Hicks ! She pats her hair, a smile on her lips.

' Oh, M-miss J-jones, would you mind . . .'

He is rather a darling. His little stammer is appealing. She wonders what his wife is like, and if his babies have that way of wrinkling their foreheads before they cry, as he does when he fumbles among the papers for a lost letter. She knows instinctively that he knows instinctively that she never imitates his stammer in the pen outside. How brown he got at Bognor.

' T-that's all, t-thank you.'

He smiles.

She smiles.

The dear . . .

Old Crouch's bell !

' That letter. Humble, Crumble, and Co. Cancel it ! Take this one ! '

What an old toad ! She goes off to type a letter to Shanghai and one to Timbuctoo. It never seems to her romantic that her fingers should spread a message nigh unto godliness to

the far corners of the earth.   Her idea of Romance
is quite different. . . .

How impossible to think of business life without
her.   She is in the City yet not of it.   Her charm
is the charm of a flower growing on an old wall.
She looks her best in a lawyer's office when, after
a climb up those dirty Georgian stairs which
lead inevitably to lawyers, she dawns on the
visitor in the splendour of her youth, graceful,
leggy, with the joyful unexpectedness of a revela-
tion.

Old Grouch's bell !

' Cancel that letter to Shanghai ! '

Very pretty the faint contempt of her shoulders.

When she escapes the others have gone to
lunch.   She takes her hat from the peg, casts a
quick look into the mirror. . . .

Old Grouch's bell !

Let him ring ! She dives down the stairs and
into that wide outside world where destinies are
arranged and dynasties founded in glances across
a tea-shop table.

Miss Jones is just flirting with bath tubs until
Fate, who has an eye for beauty, grabs her.

THE BAD GIRL

HER MOTHER refers to her, ironically, as 'miss'. Her father, when prophesying that ruin and disgrace will claim her unless she mends her ways, calls her 'your ladyship'.

'Oh !' says her mother, looking at the clock which has just struck eleven, 'so you've thought fit to come home at last, miss ! Do you know what time it is ? '

'Yes ; I went to the pictures.'

'*Pictures !* ' cries her father as incredulously as though she had said ' South Africa '. ' You've been to the *pictures* ! Do you think your mother went gadding about to the pictures night after night when she was your age ? '

'They weren't invented.'

'Don't you give me any lip ! Let me tell you this, your ladyship. Unless you behave as a respectable girl should, there's going to be trouble. I won't have my daughter talked about. Look at the paint on you ; look at your legs ! You ought to be ashamed ! One might think . . .'

'I'm no different from other girls.'

'That's no excuse ! '

'How *can* you, Hilda,' says her mother pathetically, shaking her head in sorrow over an incomprehensible child.

The Bad Girl of the Family moves philosophically about the kitchen preparing cocoa.

Things are going well. The 'row' is not half so violent as she expected. She is getting off lightly. She regards a violent clash with the old generation as the inevitable price paid by the young generation for its pleasures.

She observes her indignant parents with a sulky resentment as she goes into the scullery to find the kettle : her father, sitting in his shirt-sleeves with the evening paper and a half-empty pint bottle of stout before him on the worn table-cloth ; her mother, faded and looking much older than her age because of years spent under the tyranny of a kitchen and a washhouse. A depressing interior.

What do they know of life ? The literature she reads proves that life can be a thrilling, gay, brilliant, even romantic thing ; the cinema shows her this vivid life in progress. . . .

What a good thing she told a lie ! She had not been to 'the pictures'. She had been to the 'Palley' de Danse. That, in the opinion of her parents, is a degree nearer damnation. To admit it would have caused a real 'row', with taunts about 'followers' and frank, un-pleasant prophecies.

'Oh well. . . .'

She whistles a bar of a popular fox-trot, and her long yellow legs instinctively dance a step or two as she holds the kettle under the tap.

'A whistling woman and a crowing hen' she hears in condemnatory tones from the kitchen.

'Blast !' she whispers to the kettle.

Poor parents ; poor Hilda !

It is surely difficult to have been born practically the same shape as Helen of Troy, Cleopatra,
and Madame de Pompadour, but planted by Fate
in a dull little house in a long dull street from
which everything calculated to satisfy a sense of
beauty has been almost maliciously excluded.

It is, perhaps, a trifle easier when a generous
world offers you 15s. or £1 a week for packing
in a warehouse from 8 a.m. until 5 p.m., with
overtime at Christmas. This means that you can
beautify yourself. You can have daring ambi-
tions. You can pull long, crunchy, artificial silk
stockings on your legs in the evening, and it is
marvellous how different you feel. You can buy
a hat which you can keep ' for best '. This also
has a wonderful, improving effect on your inner
self. You can then save up gradually and buy
a costume and, after months of self-denial, a
shell-pink taffeta evening gown with a big velvet
flower on the curve of your bare shoulder. The
day will even come when you may add a pair
of pink shoes to the pink gown.

Then it is possible to steal glances at yourself
in the long mirrors of dance halls—your own
mirror shows only one half of you at a time—
and you know, beyond any doubt, that you are
a beautiful, even dazzling, young girl.

You do not analyse the tragedy that those
nearest to you, instead of praising you and
broadening your awakening sympathies, should
regard you as the Bad Girl of the Family, taunting

you as though in grasping your unassailable right to be beautiful you are doing something disreputable. Why should they regard silk as a preliminary to sin? It hurts at first when they gibe, saying that you evidently feel 'too good' for your place in society, because it never occurred to you to be a question of class : you merely wanted to look pretty.

It is good to get away from perpetual criticism, into that outside world where people like you, admire you, and say kind things to you.

In your vague life, which begins when you slam the front door, you cling from an instinct of mutual protection to a 'girl friend' of the same age with the same kind of home. You go everywhere together. You can be seen slowly parading the main street of your suburb, up and down, back and forwards, with that simulated air of an ultimate destination which people assume when they march round and round the deck of a liner. Roving bands of young men, clearly also without destination, loiter at corners and regard you with interest, sometimes whistling interrogatively.

In other strata of society there are organized occasions on which young people can satisfy this natural desire to meet and make friends, but the street is your only means of finding the companionship which youth demands. A clumsy operation called 'clicking' serves the same purpose as an introduction in less haphazard social circles.

Were you anything but an empty-headed

person you might, no doubt, take a course in something useful at a London County Council night school. Thousands of girls do ; but that is not in your line. The modern craving for tawdry excitement is as much in your blood as in that of the neurotic night club girl. You must get out, move, laugh, dance.

A husband crystallizes from the band of your admirers. He is, shall we say, as naïve as yourself, as unaware of life, the realities of life, the responsibilities of life, the possibilities of serious endeavour, and he earns barely enough for himself. In addition to his charm, he offers you an escape from a critical home.

He is the local skating champion. You visualize married life as a long, unprohibited and uncriticized skate, with perhaps a cinema thrown in, and—no one waiting up for your return !

Poor Hilda ! You soon crash into reality, but in doing so you find yourself suddenly, surprisingly and most respectably, the Good Girl of the Family.

MRS. ROBINSON

Y OU NEVER meet Mrs. Robinson in the ordinary way of business. You never even think
of her. All the other people who help to smooth
out your life are visible ; she alone lurks uncer-
tainly in the background, a vague, unconsidered
figure. . . .

It is late at night. You remember that you
have left an important letter lying about your
office ; or perhaps you have forgotten to lock
your desk. You decide to go at once and retrieve
the position.

You notice, as soon as you enter the familiar
room, that things are different. It seems that a
playful cyclone has been amusing itself there.
The waste-paper basket is standing on the table.
Other familiar objects of your daily life are
dotted about in abnormal positions, almost as
though they have been enjoying a game of
general post during your absence. They look
guilty, too. The waste-paper basket is obviously
the ringleader. He wears a look of flippant
defiance as he stands idiotically on the table, and
beside him—most extraordinary to relate—are
a pair of experienced, but morose, buttoned
boots.

Who could have imagined that on the fair
table, round which you daily gather the alert
brains of your business, should stand, with such

melancholy nonchalance, a pair of boots well acquainted with bunions?

The door opens, and there enters the room a woman carrying a sack. She is surprised to see you. It is a mutual surprise.

'Oh, sir,' she says pleasantly, but with a faint air of trespass, 'I didn't know . . .'

What she didn't know is never explained. She bustles about in a friendly way with the misplaced office equipment, lifting a chair on top of another chair, tapping the ash-tray into the waste-paper basket; and all the inanimate objects respond to her, or so you think, as a horse responds to the groom.

'It's going to rain,' remarks the visitor, lifting the buttoned boots to another position; 'my corns are jumping like anythink. . . .'

You notice that she is wearing carpet slippers.

This is Mrs. Robinson.

No women are more mysterious than the Mrs. Robinsons of London. When the City dies, as it does more or less eagerly each evening, they descend from the heights of the Hampstead ridge, from over the river, and from the eastern districts, to take over the City of London in the interest of cleanliness and good order. They come with their pails and brooms to clear up the scenes of conflict; theirs the unseen hands which wipe out the memory of dead yesterday and set the stage for to-day and another bout with Fortune.

They are not charwomen: they are cleaners. The distinction is great. A charwoman has few loyalties and no responsibility. The area of her ministrations is strictly limited. A cleaner, on the other hand, is in an almost confidential capacity. She alone of all persons may have the run of banks when the doors are closed. Down she falls on her knees every night in the temples of Midas, alone with millions which are as safe with her as with the Guardsmen at the Bank.

Every door opens before her. What secrets she learns—as learn them she must—are locked for ever in her honest heart. You never heard of a cleaner charged with blackmail; and you never will, I think. The Mrs. Robinsons of London are blessed, so it would appear, with rather less than the normal curiosity of their sex, or it may be the technique of their profession to regard the contents of even rich men's waste-paper baskets as waste paper.

Think of her in the Temple, where perhaps the arts of cleaning (and not cleaning) are seen in all their delicate finesse. Secrets lie all round her. Think of her in Whitehall surrounded by the débris of government. What must she think of us? She has never seen us, yet we must exist in her imagination by virtue of the things we throw away. No doubt she has an imaginary picture of us in her mind, pieced together over years from the scraps in our waste-paper baskets, the cigarettes we smoke, the way we have of leaving our umbrella in the office, the photographs with which we sometimes enliven the austerity of our desks and tables, and the ' perks ' we leave behind us.

It is the perquisite of a cleaner to salve from the wreckage of our days such objects as seem to her attractive or worth preserving. That is why all cleaners emerge from their cleaning carrying mysterious bundles wrapped in brown paper or sacking.

That is why you must never be surprised to see an elderly woman walking quietly down Threadneedle Street in the late hours, or the early hours, smoking the remains of a fat gold-tipped Turkish cigarette.

Such are ' perks '.

You must also show no surprise if the same honest soul boards a tramcar at the Whitehall end of the Embankment and begins to read a Blue-book entitled *Statistics of Foot and Mouth Disease throughout Eastern Europe during the Year 1926–7, with some notes of the Diseases of Cattle.*

Cleaners must own the least exciting libraries in existence.

If I were War Minister and they came to me one morning, white to the lips, to say that Secret Documents B.469 were missing, it would never occur to me to put the Secret Service on the track of the Man with the Club Foot—as in the best novels—because I would take the first tram-car to Camberwell and say to Mrs. Robinson :

' Oh, Mrs. Robinson, we're looking for some papers.'

' Nice large sheets, sir ? '

'That's it!'

'Well, bless us, if that isn't funny! I thought to myself, I thought, "If that isn't the stuff to start a real good fire I don't know what is . . . Just wait a minute! There's a bit left. . . .'

There is a lot of sound sense in Mrs. Robinson.

THE HEAD HUNTRESS

THERE is a dance in Mayfair. A striped awning runs from the stiff Georgian railings to the kerb. A thin slice of red carpet mounts to the house over the grey steps. Those pale lookers-on, who in London appear to derive some obscure delight from the pleasures of others, strain forward every time the door opens towards the bank of unseasonable flowers and green ferns which soften the austerity of the entrance hall.

' Ooh, isn't it lovely ? ' they whisper as they linger in the neighbourhood waiting for the arrival of the guests.

Behind the loveliness is Mrs. Folyot-Folyot-Browne.

In the comparative calm of her bedroom, far above the confusion of a staff augmented by flunkeys, waiters, waitresses, and others of that great army of efficients who appear instantly to control a wedding or a funeral, she wonders whether Marian will look plain to-night, as usual. A most unnatural child. Unlike other girls, who become radiant under the sting of excitement, the least thrill flings her off her balance, drives away her colour, accentuates her freckles, and generally induces a mood of disastrous dulness, a legacy from her father's family.

She was never plainer than the evening of her presentation at Court. But then she had endured the comment of an ironic populace for two awful hours. . . .

Mrs. Folyot-Folyot-Browne darts across to her daughter's room and discovers her in the last act of adornment. Her maid is fixing to the curve of her bare shoulder that one inevitable touch of colour. Bond Street has exhausted its art on her hair and her pink finger-nails. As a matter of fact, she looks almost beautiful, but pale. In a moment of gratitude Mrs. Folyot-Folyot-Browne presses her daughter's hand with maternal warmth and suggests just a touch more colour on her cheeks.

She darts back, marvellously reassured.

Mrs. Browne is that famous character in the comedy of social life : the woman whose whole energy is bent on arranging a suitable marriage for her daughter. People who write nonsense about a theoretical character known as the ' modern girl ' will tell you that such mothers are no longer tolerated. That is amusing ! There are thousands of them ! They are plotting and scheming in London at this moment. Every Royal Court fills Mayfair with them. The house agents adore them. The dressmakers thank heaven for them. The florists admire them almost as they admire love-stricken foreign noblemen.

Their only passion is husband-hunting. They have no illusions about love. They combine the commercial instincts of a Jew with the pertinacity of an insurance agent. They would crucify their self-respect on the inviting steps of St. George's, Hanover Square.

They are amusing because they are attempting to control Nature. Nature has a haphazard way of mating her creatures. Male and female in Nature are drawn mysteriously together ; rarely introduced at a party. Our smiles are born of the subconscious knowledge that inveterate match-makers are intriguing against an unaccountable force which may at any moment turn and destroy their dearest plot. They pit their cynicism, their worldly wisdom, their ambition against the wild wind of Love, which, it is well known, bloweth where it listeth.

Few people can smother a smile of satisfaction when the tables are turned on the match-maker and the girl goes off with her own man.

Nature has delivered judgment !

Nevertheless, the match-making mother is an entirely admirable and reasonable person. She shares with all mothers of unmarried daughters the feeling that her girl is potentially a social disaster or—a triumph ! This feeling is not confined to Mayfair. It exists in every street in every city and town in the land. A woman who has survived the perils of matrimony is in the position of the retired brigadier who sees his son going gaily to the war. (She knows about it all, she knows, she knows !) What helpless wrath is poured out every night of the year by mothers who observe their daughters gravitating, so it seems, towards the wrong man.

It is, however, only in Mayfair that the mother is to be seen openly making an elaborate business of a universal desire : that of picking rich and desirable husbands for their daughters. . . .

The crush downstairs is appalling. Young men and women stand jammed in rooms. A line of cars down the street brings reinforcements, with a flash of pretty legs over the red carpet and a gasp from the pale, bedraggled crowd. Who are these guests ? No one knows them all ! They have been invited in order that one man may become attracted by Marian, surely a cumbersome and clumsy affair !

Upstairs they are dancing—rather, the crowd appears to be in agitation on a square of parquet, like a pile of steel filings responding slowly and turgidly to the sweep of a magnet. In the crush somewhere is the Quarry—a detached, freehold young man with £10,000 a year now—and good prospects—a worldly character conscious of his liberty, and quite aware that the hunt is up. He can penetrate Mrs. Browne's mind and see written on her soul : ' Ten thousand, and more to come.'

No one could be more sentimental than Mrs. Browne at the sight of her daughter nestling against a bank balance ; no one less sympathetic to real love in a cottage. She believes, with Mr. P. G. Wodehouse, that ' Poverty is the banana skin on the doorstep of love '.

The mission of her life is to save Marian from slipping on it !

Marian will find herself during the season crushed up in other houses against the Quarry. They will coincide in the most skilful way at various places—at Ranelagh, Ascot, dear Lady Spindleberry's, Goodwood. Maternal eyes, as cold and calculating as eyes in the slave markets of Babylon, will observe each move in the game. Her heart will palpitate at the approach of the wrong men ; her heart will rejoice at every slight success with the right one. For all her grim determination she is helpless ; all she can do, poor dear, is to contrive propinquity and leave the rest to fate, Mr. Bollinger and moonlight.

It may be that, in due and decent course, you will read that terse announcement, so suggestive of argument and merchandise and solicitors round a table : ' a marriage has been arranged . . .'

Then Mrs. Browne, pursued by the not always sincere congratulations of other mothers who have been left at the post, will go to Deauville, there to recover from the quite too terrible strain of the London season.

' I'm a nervous wreck, my dear. . . .'

The pale crowd, charmed by distant saxophones, stands outside the house in Mayfair with the vague impression that it is on the fringe of something colourful and romantic.

M^{ANY} A country house-party has been composed round two people : the girl, and the man her mother is hunting.

When that ancient family, the Earls of Glanders and Frog, decimated by its country's wars and suffering from racial anaemia, succumbed at last to three successive spendthrifts, the estate was sold (to meet the death duties) to Mr. Archie Markham-Down, whose enormous fortune is due to those automatic handkerchief machines which stand at every street corner. You insert a coin, and out springs a neatly-folded handkerchief, male or female. The readiness with which a nation, led by spirited advertising, forsook home handkerchiefs for street handkerchiefs is one of the outstanding romances of our time. 'Sneeze —there's a Down at every corner ! ' was the famous battle-cry which led the Markham-Downs right into the heart of old England.

The history of English aristocracy since, first, the Wars of the Roses and, later, the public executioner under Henry VIII, thinned out the peerage, has been that of town wave after town wave invading the country, weathering a period of keen resentment and gradually settling down and identifying itself with the land. The *nouveaux riches* of to-day wear the coronets of to-morrow ; and why not ? They have always done so. If

117

they are decent people, and observe a proper respect for the horse, they may win their neighbours to them in a few years ; but it takes at least two generations before their villagers feel quite safe with them.

The first act of identification with the new life is marriage into an old family. This is good for all concerned.

Mrs. Markham-Down—or Milly to her friends —having decided that her daughter, Penelope, shall forge the link that is to bind new to old England, segregates several noble bachelors in her mind and sets about their pursuit with relentless but tactful ardour. There is no more earnest or determined matchmaker than the woman whose wealth is, to her, still a strictly private astonishment.

At the back of the mind of Mrs. Markham-Down is the dreadful thought that Penelope may fall in love with a commoner. Then things would be as they are. A woman who has listened to big business all her life wilts from the prospect. Some of her friends say : ' The ineffable Markham-Down is chasing the Fitzgeorge boy ! She asked—can you imagine it ?—if I'd take him down to the Towers. . . .'

Others say : ' I like old Milly ! She knows what she wants, and goes after it like a sportsman ! I'm taking Fitz down next week-end. She's got her eye on him for Penelope ; and a slice of luck for him, too. . . .'

So some week-end limousines nose their way

through the park with the dust of miles over them, there is much coming and going of the luggage van to the station, the arrival of men-servants and maidservants, the whole house is stimulated from the attics to the wine cellars—and into a gathering notable for a strange absence of good-looking young men steps Lord Fitzgeorge, the chosen, on clover and aware of it.

Is there a setting on earth more calculated to enhance the beauty of an English girl than a country house ? There is not. She can assume as many different changes of costume as a musical comedy heroine, most of them the kind of garments which English girls wear better than any women in the world.

How clumsy and inept by comparison seems the match-making of London ; the monkey-house crushes, the affected social parades ! Here, at least, the plot is hidden ! A susceptible bachelor might even forget that there is a plot : he might so easily believe that he is doing it all by himself.

In the early morning, for instance, if Fitz can rise before breakfast, he may meet the girl in a garden set in a park, and he may admire a thousand things about her in the time that it takes a herd of deer to swing round and leap into the fern. He may take breakfast with her and she may survive in his adoration. They may stand together at a sideboard choosing the same dishes ! There is a revealing intimacy about it. It is like a foretaste of felicity.

She may appear in breeches and leggings to

ride with him. If she wants him she will undoubtedly do this, because no flirtation can compare with that on horseback, knee touching knee,
so near, yet so far, so uplifted together above the
common earth ; and at the first pretended pique
off she goes ahead of him, flying like a nymph
in legend, and he must follow after, overtake and
capture her. (How strange, by the way, that
Mrs. Markham-Down should have arranged all
this ! We had almost lost sight of her benevolent
yet sinister presence !)

If the day is hot Penelope and Fitz may go to
the woods ; if it is not so hot there are tennis
courts and golf. In the evening Penelope can
become quite a different person in an evening
gown, that devastating transformation from companionship to femininity. . . .

Mrs. Markham-Down, who, sensible woman,
contrived her party with some knowledge of
astronomy, notes with the placid approval which
she bestows on the postman that the moon at its
full, enormous in the night, is lifting itself, vast
and red-gold, behind the woods.

All creatures are subject to the magic of the
moon, even members of the House of Lords.
Dynasties have been founded on moonbeams. In
moonlight a man has suddenly realized how
much a woman means to him ; the pale light has
pierced him, soaking him in powerful self-pity at
the thought of a life barren and desolate without
her. If she happens to be near at hand something is sure to be said about it. In moonlight

even a public-school education has vanished, and a man has found himself almost coherent.

'Thanks so much, dear,' writes Mrs. Markham-Down some months later, 'for your letter. He's a dear boy, and I'm sure they'll be happy. It came as a great surprise to us all. . . .'

SEA FEVER

THE GIRL who could not, if she wished, become engaged during an ocean voyage, is, I imagine, with a few rare exceptions, non-existent. Pursers tell me . . . but perhaps we had better proceed with the story. . . .

The reaction of a young man to a sea voyage seldom varies. He is leaning over the promenade deck listening to the harsh chattering of Southampton cranes; watching with perhaps idle amusement the penultimate confusion which attends the departure of an hotel on turbines. Smoke rises from the funnels, the ship throbs with a smooth, hidden life, apparent in a faint vibration in the handrail; stewards, like dentists in white jackets, dart usefully here, there and everywhere; in a few moments more the syrens will bellow, and the liner will prepare to slide away from the dockside into Southampton Water, then out to the Atlantic, its passengers isolated as surely as that gay company in the Decameron, as alone in a primitive element as the Ritz Hotel would be were it lifted two miles in the air and suspended there for seven days and seven nights.

The young man is wondering who will crystallize from the fluid crowd as a friend during the days ahead. He observes the most radiant girl he has seen in his life! She is standing with a herd of dowdy women. The syrens bellow in

hot blasts. 'Visitors ashore!' The exquisite
girl kisses the dowdy women and—goes back to
England! He is hurt, annoyed, resentful! If
only it had been she instead of that herd of
apprehensive refugees!

The land appears to perform a slow and formal
waltz round the liner, the queen among women
is left, a small waving dot at the base of an
electric crane, and he dives down to eat, meeting
at the purser's office a throng of ugly, untidy,
angry, petulant, wheedling, coy, stern, and generally unpleasant women (anyhow, he needn't know
any of them!) complaining that their cabins are
on the top deck and that they cannot stand the
wind; that they are on a lower deck, and that
they will consequently be suffocated; that an
electric fan refuses to function; that an electric
fan declines to rest, that a bathroom which is
paid for has been lost, that a bathroom which no
one will pay for has been found.

The purser behaves beautifully, making busy
little notes with a pencil, fully aware that all of
these women will be dead to argument by tea-
time. . . .

The young man savages a lamb cutlet. . . .
She was a dream girl! A queen among women!
In fact, the ideal girl met in this mad, ill-organized
jumble of life only to be lost again! He is re-
called to reality by a waiter who places before him
some exotic thing which offends his patriotism,
such as a waffle or a corn-cob.

The first forty-eight hours aboard prove to

every man how much of the beauty and brilliance
of life is due to women and the clothes they wear.
A world from which women have withdrawn
would hold no attraction. During this ghastly
period a voyager lives in such a world, drinking
too much in the coarse companionship of a
heaving bar and loathing his own sex. A hint
of the unmentionable horrors that afflict humanity
at this time is gained from the behaviour of
faithful husbands and fathers, who sneak the
paler oranges from the dessert and depart bearing bottles of Vichy and one—not more—dry
biscuit.

On the morning of the third day the young
man, now reconciled to monologue, is pacing the
hurricane deck full of good intentions. He is
feeling fit. He is eating prodigiously. He is
sleeping well. The sea is an inspiring sight.
Life is, after all, tremendously real and frightfully
earnest. He passes a girl. Quite charming !
Who is she ? he wonders. Round and round he
paces. He mounts to the boat deck. Here he
finds another girl, standing braced against the
wind. By jove, what a good-looker !

He decides to drink a cocktail before lunch.
As he is coming from the lounge he finds himself
face to face with one of those rare visions of
loveliness which dawn not twice in a lifetime.
Was it fancy, or did she really look at him with
more than a passing interest ? He feels that he
has been wrong about the ship : he has done it
an injustice !

As he lifts a large piece of ham to his mouth in the restaurant he notices (he almost blushes) the Golden Girl regarding him gravely, thoughtfully, not three tables away. She is entrancing ! He loses interest in the food. He looks round him, and lo ! in the most amazing way the whole ship has blossomed with queens of beauty as a garden in June. How on earth did it happen ? When, exactly, did it happen ? Can these be the doleful virgins who trooped aboard at Southampton like bundles of woe ? He wonders whether that grey suit of his is very creased. . . .

Now follows what is for the confirmed bachelor one of the most dangerous ordeals in life.

A voyage in a ship and the first sight of the desert affect most people in the same way. Perhaps the loneliness by which they are surrounded, a loneliness too terrible to contemplate, a loneliness so vast that it belittles mankind, draws people together in companionship as children fly from a storm to shelter. There is also the knowledge that life has been left behind. Seven days at sea are seven days outside normal existence. Human beings exiled in a ship give to each other an absorbing attention impossible anywhere else, even on a desert island.

The thing is a dangerous delusion. The sense of values is warped. A man who falls in love at sea falls fathoms deeper than he would fall on land, and in a manner different from that of any other phase of the phenomenon, for does he not retain a most remarkable buoyancy which

125

enables him to emerge like a diver with surprising rapidity at the smell of the first land fog?

Liner love can be compared only to those romances which afflict young people at a masquerade ball where, isolated in a little space of unreality, they conceive a poetic fancy which dies, if not with the dawn, possibly with the dawn after that! The crew of a ship, immune from sea magic and engrossed with the task of earning their living, observe the effect on their charges as men awake, and in their right senses, might watch the beclouded actions of people under the influence of opium.

Our young man then, if he has not, before the dawning of the seventh day, carelessly become engaged to several women in his enthusiasm, discovers himself under the hardly less complicated spell of one. Her slightest action is vital. She occupies the Universe. There has never been a girl like her. There never will be. She is his one escape from boredom. Every moment without her is an ache. He follows, anxious to serve her. He is a slave as no man, no matter how willing, could be on land. He crams months of kind deeds and happy thoughts into a few days. Should she send a cable, it seems to him as important as if she had won the Nobel Prize for literature.

He sits wallowing in indiscriminate adoration as she commits the folly of singing at the ship's concert. On the sanity of land her version of ' I passed by your window ' might not have wrecked his passion, but it would hardly have caused him to demand an encore. None of us likes to see his dear ones behaving foolishly. At sea, however, he sits with dewy eyes, his heart vibrating to her voice as a harp under the fingers of a master.

If he could keep away from the boat deck after a dance ! Vain thought. The moment he places his foot on the companion-way the night air is filled with the ghosts of salad bowls and ink-stands.

Up there under the stars the wind is sighing through the rigging, and there is a musical sound, a queer, hollow moan of wind in the high, hot funnels ; and now and then the whole spangled firmament tilts slightly and remains so for a second, then swings gently, so gently and smoothly, to the other side. There is the ting-ring of navigating bells from the bridge, and the tactful cough of the night-watchman, the spluttering stammer of the wireless, and the soft, regular sough of the water as the great ship cleaves her way.

In the inspired imagination of the young man, R.M.S. *Eupeptic* appears to resemble a golden arrow flying through the timeless fields of Paradise.

The day after the liner docks in New York the following headline appears in an evening paper :

ENGLISH BARONET MEETS BRIDE ON LINER. ' HAPPIEST MAN ON EARTH,' SAYS SIR JONES.

Or—or he may stand, a little puzzled, watching her retreat in the crowds, feeling slightly surprised and dazed, wondering what exactly happened to him in that ship, for when her feet touched land she somehow became different, or surely he would not have found himself gazing with the eye of the instinctive bigamist at that other really astonishing girl in the green hat.

THE GOLFER is the ideal husband. He is
a man of steady habit and fine patience,
otherwise he could not play the game. He is a
man of some substance, otherwise he could not
afford to play it. He has made some position
for himself, otherwise he could not disappear
from his work with such frequency. He is generally a man of a highly desirable age, a man from
whom the fret and fever of youth have departed,
for golf is the malady of the mature.

Observe how rashly the good things of life are
squandered in one place ! As if this catalogue
of qualities were not sufficient, he possesses that
ideal attribute in a husband—a genius for dis-
appearance !

Some men love their homes with a concentrated
and adhesive passion which induces in some
women a desire to scream, to run away, to swear,
to drink, to be beaten and ill-used. Such unfail-
ing loyalty to that which is theirs, such suffocating
satisfaction with life, such a tender concern with
all the intimate details of domestic life, and,
above all, such unbearable ubiquity, cause men
of this type to be appreciated only when they
have taken their first, and last, long journey from
home.

It is not strange that women do not love the
perfect man. Perfection leaves nothing to the

imagination. How often, I wonder, have women prayed in the secret depths of their hearts that their husbands might develop small vices?

Now the golfer produces all the phenomena of vice without becoming vicious. He is away from home as carelessly and as often as the philanderer. Yet in all the long records of the Divorce Court has there been one co-respondent cited as 'a golfer'? There has not! Golfers are the most moral of men. They are de-bunkered of passion. Then, again, the temper of a golfer is as uncertain as that of a drinker. His generosity, when flushed with victory, is as sudden and magnificent as that of a man who is trying to soothe a conscience.

Add to this the astonishing fact that the golfer is impervious to boredom (otherwise he could not play golf) and you have a man who will not only never revolt against marriage, but will also bring to that adventure all the qualities that compose happiness.

A golf course on a sunny morning!

What finer setting for a girl? (After all, the setting is so important!) She wears a tight little hat of felt, a jumper and a small tube of tweed cloth. One of the marvels of this life is the heart-breaking beauty which Englishwomen—and Englishwomen alone of all the millions of women on the earth's surface—can contrive from a handful of felt and two yards of tweed.

The dress of the man accentuates his masculinity (for no woman would be found dead in plus fours). The woman on a golf course is supremely

feminine. It is as if her sex is underlined in red
ink. As she grips the turf with her feet and
leans forward to play a stroke, she is distractingly
interesting. The swing of her body, too, would
be painfully beautiful seen once only in a lifetime. Then, as she stands for one second before
she turns for admiration or sympathy, queerly
twisted, maintaining her stance, her club flung
backward, eager, flushed, looking forward to the
next tee with narrowed eyes and parted lips—a
lovely second in which she is utterly wrapped up
in herself and concentrated on her own success—
how lovable she is ; and how completely satis-
factory !

She plays so badly, too. That is one of her
greatest attractions. Few really attractive women
play golf well. This would be intolerable. Consequently the man is sensible of his superiority.
He can hit farther—not perhaps straighter—and
this flatters the boastful little boy in him. This
is necessary for his self-respect. Also, consider
the moral effect on a man who has been con-
sistently beaten by every one when he encounters
at length some one whom he can patronize !
(It is perhaps a little late in the history of the
world to remind women that the consuming
vanity of the male must always be considered in
dealings with this complex sex. When wounded
the beast is stupid, when flattered it will dance
to almost any tune.)

So the man, taking a mighty swipe, hits an
unusual 150 yards.

Her eyes are more than a reward ; they are a testimonial. With a little, nervous shrug, she says :

' Oh, dear, I wonder if I'll ever be able to hit a golf ball. . . .'

' You're improving with every stroke,' he says grandly.

' But I'm not ! I'm terribly bad ! I try to copy you, but—oh, I don't know ! '

She takes a weak swing and does a 140 yards !

' Not too bad ! ' he says. ' Now, look here, if you'll grip more with your left . . .'

Her eyes, her big eyes, are fixed on his manly, helpful presence with an almost childish desire to become as great as he.

' Show me ! ' she says appealingly.

He places his hands over her small hands :

' Now that's better ! '

' Thanks ! '

' Now take a swing ! '

' Fine ! '

' Honest ? '

' Splendid ! '

' I give you full marks for patience ! ' she laughs.

In a brain congested with dark thoughts of Abe Mitchell, St. Andrews, niblicks, drivers, and putters, is lit a faint glimmer of admiration. As he plays his next stroke half a pound of rich farm-land descends over them, confetti like :

' I *say*, I'm terribly sorry ! '

' Oh, how lovely ! ' she laughs gaily, wiping

her left eye, ' to know that *even you* can make a mistake ! '

' I can't think how . . . please let me . . .'

He takes her small handkerchief and, approaching close to her, places one hand on her shoulder and tries not to blind her, as she stands obediently, trying hard to endure the pain of his blundering assault on her eye.

' There, that's better ! ' she lies bravely. ' It's out ! Only a bit of grit or something ! '

Impatient men approach, waiting in relaxed attitudes, their expressions full of contempt. These men were once his friends ! Now and then comes a sound like that of a colossal cow : ' Fore ! ' But he knows now that two is company. Let them wait !

The intimacy of the deep bunker. The distant hoarse murmur of the English language from adjacent bunkers. The sky overhead. Larks shivering and trilling high above :

' Your shot ! '

' Oh, is it ? '

She misses.

' Bad luck ! '

He breaks his niblick !

' Great —— Scott ! '

' You know,' she whispers, ' although I'm no good at all, it does help me to go round with you.'

' You *are* good,' he says earnestly, then his native honesty asserts itself, and he adds, ' and you'll be jolly good soon. . . .'

There is tea, that intoxicating beverage, in the club house ; and then the drive home :

' Tell me,' she asks thoughtfully. ' I've been thinking ! Did Abe Mitchell ever drive farther than you did from the third tee ? '

His hand leaves the wheel ! Wild emotion flares up in his heart. His brain is lit with splendid fires. This is the first time he uses the word ' darling ! '

After marriage the wife can either sell her clubs or give them to an unmarried sister. It is unnecessary, and, in fact, unwise, for her to endure this game again.

BEHIND THE SCENES

WE ARE all amateur actors. Napoleon was the greatest amateur actor of his time, Borgia of his, Caesar of his. Some of us, however, content with a smaller stage, hire the town hall. . . .

In every suburb, and in every provincial town, men and women, who lead otherwise blameless lives, meet together in the evenings in a haphazard conspiracy to produce a play. They are bound together by a feeling that they have been wrongly cast, but that it 'will be all right on the night'. 'The Night', of course, refers to that occasion when the Cats' Home is to be placed for ever beyond the pale of financial anxiety.

Even Mr. Hannen Swaffer has not yet decided why people who are not obliged to do so produce plays. The leading motive cannot be a love for humanity, nor yet a compassion for dumb creatures, because it has been proved time and again that when the hall, the flood lights, the limelights, the costumes, the programmes and the stage hands have been paid, the Cats' Home remains in the same unprotected condition.

The psychologist would probably cite vanity as the ruling motive. A more tolerate investigator might put forward the guess that romance will out. After all there is a streak of heroism in most men which is unsatisfied by a normal day's work in the offices of the Gas Light and Coke Company. None of the ordinary hobbies satisfies this ache. Tennis may be all right for the thoughtless. That is purely physical. Amateur acting leads straight into the land of make-believe. It almost seems that for one night we have changed places with the person we ought to be. That, no doubt, is why you occasionally interrupt a pale cashier or a mild shop assistant in the act of muttering beneath his breath :

'The devil damn thee black, thou cream-fac'd loon.
Where got'st thou that goose look?'

In a few hours he will be Macbeth.

Like unto the sands of the sea are the happy marriages which trace themselves to an amateur dramatic society. These can be abiding unions. An amateur actor makes an excellent husband because to him one person is an audience, which is at once the charm and the tragedy of marriage. (The Divorce Court proves that the professional actor is more exacting.) He has an intimate acquaintance with the great characters of romance. He is, therefore, adaptable. He is used to placing himself in other people's boots, tights, doublets, and hose. He is therefore sympathetic. He is rarely ill at ease. He can be relied on to handle those situations in domestic life where a little flourish ('shouts within and trumpets sound', as Shakespeare puts it) is not only desirable but indispensable.

He is so accustomed to the feeling that some

one is about to forget and let him down that
he is in a continual condition of helpful apprehension. He is also coherent. His language is
stimulated by contact with the great masters.
This, of course, can become tiring, but a clever
woman can handle a small detail of this
kind. Above everything, he is well balanced.
All ill-balanced amateur actors become pro-
fessionals.

He is, in fact, that rare and desirable character
from a woman's standpoint ; the man who is
accustomed to short exhibition flights into fantasy,
none of them long enough or dangerous enough
to imperil his sense of reality. Compared with
a whole-time artist, he is a captive balloon
anchored most comfortingly to a broker's office
or a bank. He may murder the princes in the
Tower at night, but he can always be relied on
to catch the eight-forty-five in the morning. . . .

And the amateur actress !

It is practically impossible for a pretty girl to
play Rosalind, Juliet, Portia, Jessica, Viola, Olivia,
Miranda, or Titania without seriously wounding
the heart of Orlando, Romeo, Bassanio, Lorenzo,
the Duke, Ferdinand, or Oberon. The effect
may be even more devastating, extending to
' guards, watchmen, attendants, and messengers ',
even to those humble, effaced characters suggested only at the time of their frequent departures
by the comprehensive word ' exeunt '.

Amateur Shakespeare is frequently a matri-
monial agency. And what more lovely than to

10   137

be brought together by the best blank verse in the world. . . .

A rehearsal is in progress. The actors, or such of them as have remembered to come, are sitting sadly about the dull schoolroom in silent communion with the efforts of the still-life class and the map of Europe. One man mutters in a deep voice, over and over again, towards a crayon sketch of a carrot :

> 'Some God direct my judgment : Let me see ;
> I will survey the inscriptions back again !
> What says the leaden casket ? '

In a cleared space the producer, a young, forceful, and unpopular man, is taking Lorenzo and Jessica through the love scene of Act V. Lorenzo has obviously just met Shakespeare for the first time, and has disliked him intensely. He is a young, sleek man with motor-cycles in his soul. He repeats his lines unwillingly as if reciting disastrous market quotations to a violent employer :

'Stop !' cries the producer. 'I say, old man, do put a bit of life into it.'

'How do you mean ?' asks Lorenzo.

'Well, dash it, you're supposed to be in love with her ! Go back again to " Who comes so fast in silence of the night ? " . . .'

Jessica is charming. Any man might forget after two rehearsals that she is Miss Brown of 'Balmoral.' In fact, the producer has already done so. He wishes that Lorenzo would fall out of

the cast, but, unfortunately, only in extreme cases
of feeble-mindedness can people be expelled
from amateur theatricals. (Incidentally, Lorenzo's only attachment to Shakespeare is Miss
Brown of 'Balmoral'!)

'Now, look here!' cries the producer, 'this is
the way.'

He strides over to Jessica, places his arm on
her shoulder, and walks a space with her through
the 'moonlit garden', speaking in a rich, romantic
voice. You can almost hear the nightingales.
Then he kisses her.

She blushes. The young man tries to look
intelligently interested. It's a bit thick, he
thinks, but it's only acting! She continues to
blush. Quite unexpectedly the producer blushes!
(Portia in the background sitting on a desk nudges
her waiting-maid, Nerissa!)

Ho-ho!

Well, I never!

At the next rehearsal Lorenzo has revised his
technique. The producer is moved to restrain
him!

'Don't eat poor Jessica!' he says sternly,
blushing again. 'There's no need, you know!'

'But you told me to be romantic.'

'Yes, but not hungry! Remember, it's a
calm, poetic scene.'

Jessica, all pretty confusion, flickers her thanks.
The youth is stupid. Now, if only the producer . . .

The night! No work done all day! Gas

Light and Coke affairs forgotten, banking aban-
doned! A message from Lorenzo : 'Spill from
motor-cycle. Ankle sprained. Can't play!'

What a blessing, thinks the producer, we are
the same height !

From the local paper : 'Mr. Herbert Jones,
who produced the play, stepped at short notice
into the part of Lorenzo, where he acquitted
himself admirably except in the love scene. Here
he seemed overcome by diffidence, and the voice
of the prompter was loud in the land.'

The same paper, six months later : 'Among
the wedding presents was a handsome set of
Shakespeare's works from the Westfield Dramatic
Society.'

That is how it happens. People of sensibility
dabble in amateur theatricals at their own risk.

ABOUT PLACES

A MAN OF THE WORLD

A YOUNG MAN stood behind the counter of a tourist office handling the migrants with the calm touch of an efficient god. Neat, swift, with fingers moving expertly through alien Bradshaws, he spoke to the crowd which pressed about him as if from the high mountain peak of some superior plane of technical knowledge. Other men were baffled and undone by passionate old ladies from Putney who, tearing down the Southend excursion bills, wandered angrily into the Atlantic booking department to demand additional enlightenment. The young man received these women as they were shooed out by his colleagues, and he soothed them, settled their problems for them so that their fury abated—so that they would have taken tea out of his hand !

'What a nice young man !'

Younger women looked back and said : 'What a perfect darling !'

The young man was handsomely sunburnt. There was that atmosphere about him which surrounds only the globe-trotter. While he remained essentially English, he had absorbed the graces of a dozen nations.

In the winter, when people go south to Italy and Egypt, hardened travellers have stood amazed at this young man's knowledge of the world. There is no city on the face of the earth which he does not know intimately. He could draw you a street plan of Trieste as easily as he could sketch you a map of Moscow. He is like some unique human signpost pointing now to Brighton and the next moment to Bagdad. Men admire him for his mind ; women because there is that indefinite something about him which inspires the beholder with the belief that such a man could never get into the wrong train or receive the wrong change. Husbands who lose passports, become fussy about the luggage, who rebuff the innocent foreigner and suspect the kind-hearted, have often in the secrecy of the wifely heart been compared unfavourably with the Young Man in the Ticket Office Who Knows the World and the Way of It.

You will gather that the sight of him handling an Easter crowd must have been a lesson in the right application of knowledge. But it was not worthy of him. A man who knows the one place in Mecca where you must drink coffee is wasted on the Margate sector. Still, he was wonderful.

He listened gravely to the surprising man who, simply because he was going to Paris, had lost his lean legs in a gigantic pair of plus fours (these things do happen, possibly by arrangement with the French comic papers !), and he told him with mechanical swiftness that the train which leaves Calais at twelve-forty-five slides into the Gare du Nord at sixteen-twenty-five. There was almost a fatherly solicitude in the tone of this young man as he leaned forward to assure a pettishly childlike grandfather that bath chairs are a natural feature of the Bournemouth landscape ; a moment after he was just like a son putting his arm round his mother as he advised a grey-haired woman to take the three-forty-nine from Paddington so that she might drink tea on her way to St. Ives. And then he turned with the same suave, methodical patience to a girl.

She was the kind of girl that young men always hope to—and never do—rescue from bandits on the Riviera express. She had been waiting a long time, with her large blue eyes fixed appealingly on that paragon. But the Young Man Who Knows the World heard her as if she were a talking doll, and then without a suspicion of gallantry informed her that if she really must go via Saronno there were seven good trains from Milan to Como. She thanked him and used her eyes ; but the young man was talking about Brightlingsea to a man with long white whiskers. Oh, rare, remarkable young man !

When the last migrating spinster had departed, the Young Man Who Knows the World took down his hat and prepared for home.

Somewhere in Brixton is a little house in a road of little houses which are so much alike that wives place bowls of goldfish and aspidistras in the windows in order that their husbands may find the way back to the right home. To this house went the Man Who Knows the World. He opened the door with a latchkey, and you, if you only knew him professionally, would have expected to see a pile of Saratoga trunks, a carved table, a bit of Chinese ivory, and perhaps a few of those hideous walking-sticks which attach themselves to men who wander. But no. In the little hall there was nothing but a hatstand waiting hungrily with outstretched mahogany hands for hats.

He listened; then tiptoed to a room in which a fair, fluffy young woman was rocking a child to sleep.

'Hallo, Perce!' she said. 'Had a busy day, dear?'

'Only so so,' replied the Man Who Knows the World. 'Margate and Blackpool and all that sort of thing. What's for supper?'

'Sardines.'

It must add variety to a life spent advising strangers to sample the caviare of little-known restaurants on the Continent to come home to sardines. The young man smiled and said, 'Good.'

As they sat down to supper he appeared to be taking very little interest in the blue dress with the white piping.

'And only forty-seven-and-six, too.'

'Effie,' he remarked suddenly, 'I *would* love to take you to Paris this Whitsun.'

'Poor old boy,' she whispered. 'It's such a shame you've never been abroad! You do so

146

want to travel, dear, don't you? Perhaps if you hadn't married me. . . .'

He went over and kissed her.

' Perce,' she asked, 'where are we going for the holidays this year?'

' Oh, the usual, I expect.'

' I'm so sick of Southend,' she pouted. ' Can't we manage Ramsgate?'

The Man Who Knows the World got up, paced the room thoughtfully, then, turning to her with an indecision never shown when dealing with other people's travels, said :

' I'll see.'

FIFTY ALMOST naked women wearing head-
dresses of ostrich plumes group themselves
against the transformation scene like flies in a
spangled web. Some are mounted high on the
stage; others, leaping on the white knees or
the white shoulders of their companions, stretch
out white arms and white legs until the pyramid
of powdered flesh is built up and linked together.
Then, with the band crashing into a finale,
electric lights make the scene even more vulgar and
silly; and the curtain slides down. The drunken
Englishman in the next stall goes on applauding.
This, he thinks, is Paris.

During the *entr'acte* there is a rush to the little
tables of the room outside. The place is almost
fogged with the blue smoke of cigars and
cigarettes. Only a few people can seize tables;
the rest stand about jammed together as tight
as the crowd in Frith's ' Derby Day '. Sallow,
dreary waiters, distinguished by a weary air of
studied insolence, push through the crowd holding
trays of drink. People pull them by their long
aprons as they pass, in an attempt to catch their
attention. The bar presents an undignified chaos
of backs and stretching arms as men shove, fight
and elbow for little glasses of brandy. And high up
in a gallery, but completely drowned by the babel
of hundreds of people talking against each other,

an orchestra plays with malicious savagery in
the grim determination to keep the party going.

A young Englishman stands out vividly from
the rather tawdry, middle-class crowd, because
he is well bred and perfectly dressed in a tail-coat.
Beside him is a pretty English girl, who is obviously his bride. He shoulders a way for her
through the French crowd, very embarrassed,
touching his sandy moustache nervously with
finger and thumb, glaring with the superiority
of his kind at everything near him, thinking that
it would have been great fun had he been alone,
wondering if it is quite the place to bring Joan.

An enormous flaxen strumpet like a galleon in
full sail, unaware of Joan in the crush, seizes
the bridegroom by the arm with : ' 'Allo, *ma
chérie!* You luf me much, yes?' And the Englishman, more ashamed than ever, shakes off the
offending arm and pushes more vigorously into
the throng.

The room gets hot to the point of suffocation.
The noise becomes more violent. It is easy to
pick out the Englishmen. Most of them are
tourists or commercial travellers suffering from
the delusion that they are seeing life in the ' gay
City '. They would be surprised if you suggested
to them that it is all very old-fashioned. But
Paris after dark is old-fashioned.

Three obese and powdered women, of a type
now so obsolete that it is believed they expired the
day the Leicester Lounge was closed, regard with
fantastic concern the glass of *crème de menthe*

which a waiter in one of his passing moments
has spilt over a white evening gown.

'It will come out, dearest,' you can hear
them say.

'Oh, that careless *crétin*, that Albert!'

An elderly Englishman clearly labelled Surbiton
gives them something else to think about. He
sits down nervously on the red plush seat near
the tons of *houri* and gazes round as if hoping that
none of his fellow-directors can see him. The
icy barrier of his reserve appears to be melting
under the influence of whisky and expressions in-
tended to suggest amourousness—which, however,
are merely fatuously maternal. So large and
established mothers in Birmingham and Bradford
gaze at sons of eighteen.

Frenchmen with square beards talk together
at express speed, their heads close, sometimes
leaning back and accentuating a remark by
curving the right hand and seizing an imaginary
pinch of air like a man taking snuff. And
sometimes an old Frenchman will say something
witty, placing a finger against his nose and half-
winking in the most knowing manner.

And it comes over you gradually that you
might be your grandfather having a night out
in Paris. Red plush, brandy, fat women, noise,
the spurious air of gallantry, the march from
Aïda—nothing has changed. Something in your
blood recognizes it, as it used to recognize the
exciting squalidity of the old *Café Royal*.

As you look round the music hall, you expect

to see in the crowd an elegant figure in check
trousers leaning on a malacca cane, his Lordship
of Dundreary, and you wait for the doors to
swing open at any moment for Trilby and Little
Billie.

The orchestra strikes up a fox-trot, playing it
clumsily and unsurely. No ; no ; that is still to
come ! That is a prophecy. Let them stick to
Verdi, for the world is still in the eighteen-sixties,
' Edward P.' is setting forth on his great career
as the almost life-long Prince of Wales, and outside in the Paris streets there are surely hansom-
cabs.

WHITE TEMPLES

The door of the restaurant near the Forum
Trajanus was suddenly flung wide, and in
rushed a crowd of excited men. They carried
something to a central table, shouting and laughing. Guests stopped eating. The waiters left
their tasks. Half the restaurant was soon gathered
curiously round the invaders, laughing and joking
about the thing they had brought in with them.
It was a snowball !

I pulled aside the curtain and saw that
snow was falling over Rome, flickering in the
light of its lamps, whitening the streets and
settling softly on arch and pillar. The most
dignified city in Europe was transformed suddenly
into a city of urchins. A man in an opera hat
on his way to the Constanza Theatre picked up
a handful of snow which he pretended to throw
at his friend. He did not instinctively make a
hard ball of it as any northern man would have
done : he just picked up the softness and threw
it in the air where the wind blew and scattered it.

And I remembered what it was like when we
were children to awaken in the night and see
snow falling on tree and field. How exciting it
was. How exquisitely the snow transformed a
well-known world. It was as though the earth,
in tune with our youth, was 'dressing up' for a
charade.

I went out into the streets where flakes spun and whirled in the night. All Rome was out of doors marvelling at it. It seemed to me so strange that a city which has known so much should be so moved by snowflakes.

I came upon a group of elderly Romans solemnly rolling an enormous snowball down the Capitoline Hill. Even the wolves in the cage beneath the Capitol sat on their haunches with their muzzles against the wire-netting watching the strange thing that had happened to their city. The thrill of phenomena was so clearly printed on Rome that I remembered those lines in which Shakespeare describes the signs and portents that heralded the death of Caesar. Says Calpurnia to Caesar :

'A lioness hath welped in the streets ;
  And graves have yawned and yielded up their dead ;
  Fierce, fiery warriors have fought upon the clouds
  In ranks and squadrons and right form of war
  Which drizzled blood upon the Capitol ;
  The noise of battle hurtled in the air,
  Horses did neigh, and dying men did groan,
  And ghosts did squeak and squeal about the streets.
  O Caesar ! these things are beyond all use,
  And I do fear them.'

Rome on this night of snow knew, it is true, the fun of phenomena, but the effect on the population was much the same. Men and women went laughing through the white streets saying, in the words of Shakespeare :

'Cassius, what night is this ? '
  'A very pleasant night for honest men.'
  'Who ever knew the heavens menace so ? '

I found myself at the Colosseum. Here was a sight few men have seen. Snow outlined the tiers of seats from which crowds once watched chariot races and death. A carpet of purest white was spread over that arena which has known so much red ; and against the whiteness stood up the gaunt cross that commemorates the first saints.

Most beautiful of all was the Forum against dizzy clouds of snow. Broken architrave and shattered pillar seemed to form again and become whole, so that one looked through the white mist on a vision of ancient Rome alive again. Once more the Forum was a glory of white marble, and I saw in the whirling flakes above the Via Sacra the sheeted ghosts of saint and emperor. Decay was eliminated by the even whiteness of the snow, which painted out the ruins and created an uncanny illusion of life, so that in the darkness and through the flurries of snow the varied crowds which Rome once drew to her streets from every corner of the world moved on between white temples silent as the dead.

The snow fell all that night and on the day following, so that old men, raking their memories, said that nothing like it had been seen in Rome for more than forty years.

HOW ROME AWAKENS

IF YOU would know a city you must prowl round in the temporary innocence of its dawn. You must wait until it stirs slightly in the first winds of day, seeming to shiver a little in returning consciousness. I have watched—like some one sitting at a bedside—how London, Edinburgh, Dublin, Paris, Brussels, Berlin, Vienna, Cairo, Jerusalem, and many other great cities stretch themselves, yawn and open their arms to returning life. No two cities awaken in precisely the same way; and Rome, I think, has the most remarkable *réveille* in Europe.

In the winter it is only half light at 6 a.m. and dark at five. The streets of Rome are empty. The familiar temples and colonnades which a man has known since he was a child in books or hanging over the vicar's mantelpiece, stand in a grey hush, a vague mist over them like the dust from the wheels of ghostly chariots. In the queer mix-up of Rome they stand sandwiched between furtive buildings whose ominous shutters might open to reveal Juliet or—an assassin with a bomb!

The sound of Rome is not yet the staccato clang of car bells, but the splash of fountains. The only movement is the slide of water over marble basins, the whiteness of flung jets, the thin half-circles spouting from the bronze mouths of nymph or Triton. The square Renaissance palaces, their lower windows iron-barred like prison cells, lie, so it seems in this grey hour, in an old dream of daggers and fair women.

A cat with the expression of a Borgia slinks from the shadows on some grim, premeditated deed.

The east flushes. Colour comes back. Temples and palaces stand with roofs in the first light and feet in the last shadows. The ' tawny ' Tiber is silver under dark bridges, and—listen— a bell ! The churches are awake. Rome is one enormous church, therefore Rome is awake ! The solemn bells call to early Mass. Rome's first thought is of God.

And as I go on through the streets, meeting the first tramcar with its cargo of sallow sleepy faces, I see the long lines of country chariots coming in over roads whose names sound to a man like the beating of a sword against a shield. They are queer carts mounted on high blue wheels and drawn by loose-limbed and reluctant mules.

A gorgeous umbrella, rather like some enormous sea shell, curves from back to front, forming a pretty shelter for the driver, his wife and his family. Here and there is a slower cart pulled by white oxen. Gay tassels shake over their broad heads. They bear barrels of Frascati. They rumble over the stones as to some festival of Bacchus.

It is suddenly light. The tip of the obelisk in the square is gold in sunlight.

What makes Rome in the morning so remarkable? It is like a garrison town! You are for two hours conscious only of the Church. Modern things have not returned to the streets. You are in the Middle Ages, among monks and friars and slow wine-carts and bells. The streets become a parade ground for little ecclesiastical squads. Monks go barefoot girdled with cord, hands folded in rough sleeves like Chinese mandarins; Sisters of Mercy return to their convents from some early mission—the collecting of broken bread from hotel kitchens, most likely.

Most notable of all are the seminarists. Thousands of young men from every country in the world are learning to be priests and missionaries. The English wear black gowns; the Scottish, violet gowns with red girdles and black cloaks; the Irish, black with red lappets and binding; the Germans and Hungarians, red; the Spanish, black with blue girdles; the Belgians, black with red seams; the Poles, black with green girdles; the Americans, black with blue girdles and blue linings.

It is a League of Nations on parade. These young men behave like soldiers. There is no sloppy lounging off to a lecture as in a University town; each squad parades with discipline under a leader and marches off two by two, and one umbrella between each half section!

A monseigneur, hatted and in black, crosses the square briskly like a colonel on his way to a kit inspection!

This activity is by 9 a.m. submerged beneath the normal traffic of a great city. It is there, but it is not visible ! The streets fill, the shops open, the motor-cars become jammed in the Corso and the Via Condotti. But just as in Aldershot you can never be unconscious of the army, so in Rome, if you have seen this city awaken, you can never be unconscious of the undeviating discipline of the Church.

Somewhere out of sight the thousands of young men who paraded before breakfast are going through their Catholic exercises. And until you know this you have not seen Rome. These are the legions which Rome has been sending out for centuries.

The young men are turned out labelled Rome as clearly as men are turned out labelled Winchester or Eton. They are the recruits of Roman Catholicism ; and I can recommend no more depressing sight to an anti-Catholic than a 6 a.m. tour through the ' Eternal City '.

There are Protestants who will regard the glimpse of Rome as the most dangerous thing in the world. There are men who will watch the holy platoons with the eyes of John Knox. I merely report without comment one of the great facts of Europe : a first hour of daylight which reveals an army on parade.

THE TOMB OF CHARLES EDWARD
STUART

WHEN BONNIE PRINCE CHARLIE'S star sank for ever at Culloden he escaped to Skye, where Flora Macdonald hid him. A French man-o'-war took him to the Continent. Forty years later he died in Rome with the title of ' Charles III, King of England, Scotland, France and Ireland ', but with no country and no friends. He is buried in St. Peter's.

I rose early to visit his tomb. It was hardly light. Rome was awakening to the sound of bells. In its many churches crowds knelt before altars at which priests in embroidered chasubles moved through the intricate ritual of the Mass. I crossed the most impressive square in Europe and entered St. Peter's.

The tremendous church was a chill tomb of marble where vast sepulchral figures of saint and Pope, escorted by dimpled cherubim, leaned out of shadows to make the sign of the Cross over the centuries. The eighty-nine little flames lay like a field of yellow flowers round the tomb of that saint whose faults Christ loved ; and from side chapels came the chanting of Latin, the scent of incense, and the ringing of bells at the elevation of the Host.

I found the tomb of Charles Edward in the left aisle.

Life is not always artistic. Bonnie Prince Charlie should have died among the clans at Culloden, or at least after his adventures in Skye. One of life's tragedies is the ease with which a man can outlive his reputation.

Charles Edward's gallant fight for the throne of his ancestors in the year 1745 was the last flicker of authentic romance in a world which already contained James Watt. The greatest tribute to him is perhaps the fact that we think of him never as elderly or dissipated, or as wandering mysteriously about Europe in an atmosphere of failure and embarrassment, but we see him always in his kilt of Stuart tartan striding through the heather to the splendour of a lost cause. He did, in a sense, die at Culloden because no ugliness of later life can touch him ; he will always be 'Bonnie' Prince Charlie.

The romance of the House of Stuart, which is the appealing romance of misfortune wedded to good looks, wrung many a tear from the later Georges when the crown sat easily on their heads. In fact these princes inherited a Highland complex, which showed itself not only in fancy-dress balls, so that one is almost persuaded that they might have been good Jacobites had they not answered the call of the Protestant succession ! Those appealing Stuarts !

I suppose many an English Protestant who has shed his blood for King George V has stood before this tomb in St. Peter's with a white cockade in his soul. It is rather curious ! I placed a white flower on the tomb, and it looked, I thought, rather like those cockades which Mrs. Secretary Murray, sitting a horse and holding a drawn sword, handed out in the courtyard of Holyrood while the young man who called himself Prince of Wales smiled down from an upper window.

The Stuart monument is shaped like an Egyptian pylon. It is surmounted by the arms of England and by an inscription in Latin which gives to Prince Charles and his father the titles denied to them in life. On either side of the closed door the only two naked women in St. Peter's stand in mournful attitudes. They are angels with perfect figures. Canova made them.

When you look at these figures you notice that they are stained from the waist to the knee. This stain is the shadow of a metal kilt ! It appears that during the reign of Leo XIII the superb curves of Prince Charlie's mourners attracted too much attention, so that the Pope ordered them to be concealed by a kilt of metal painted to resemble a marble drapery ! So they remained until the last Pope, Pius X, took pity on them and undressed them.

In the crypt of St. Peter's, beneath this marble monument, are the actual tombs of the last Stuarts—Prince Charlie's father, the Old Pretender, Prince Charlie and his younger brother, Cardinal York, who extinguished the Jacobite cause for ever under the sacred sterility of a red hat.

You descend into a dim catacomb. An elderly

Italian goes with you, jingling a bunch of keys and switching electric lights on and off as he keeps up an animated historical commentary. All round you shine the white faces of dead Popes carved in stone. There is a gleam of gold mosaic and a glitter of bronze. You are beneath the central dome of St. Peter's. The saint's body lies in a gilded shrine. The pavement you tread has known the sandals of Constantine and Charlemagne. Out of the shadows of Roman arch and from the gloom of low vaulting might sound, it seems, at any moment a great blast of trumpets. The darkness is so full of history that its cold silence frightens you. You are in the womb of the modern world.

The guide switches on a light and leads you to the three Stuart tombs, big sarcophagi built into the wall and unadorned save for the names of the three unfortunate men who lie there. On Bonnie Prince Charlie's tomb are two bunches of heather, one white and one purple, and both brittle with age.

As I stood there the words of an old song which was sung in Gaelic in 1745 rushed into my mind, and I gripped the elderly Italian, who had tried to tell me about the Stuarts, firmly by the arm and let him have it :

‘ Come o'er the stream, Charlie, dear Charlie, brave Charlie,
Come o'er the stream, Charlie, and dine with Maclean ;
And though you be weary, we'll make your heart cheery,
And welcome our Charlie and his loyal train.

162

We'll bring down the track deer, we'll bring down the
　　black steer,
　The lamb from the breckan, and doe from the glen ;
The salt sea we'll harry, and bring to our Charlie
　The cream from the bothy, and curd from the pen.

O'er heath bells shall trace you the maids to embrace you,
　And deck your blue bonnet with flowers of the brae ;
And the loveliest Mari in all Glen M'Quarry
　Shall lie in your bosom till break of the day. . . .

Come o'er the stream, Charlie, dear Charlie, brave Charlie,
　Come o'er the stream, Charlie, and dine with Maclean.'

The elderly Italian, with the instinctive feeling
of his race, stood silently beside me in the half-
darkness, having understood nothing except the
feeling of it. But a little wind out of Scotland
must have come to St. Peter's, for we suddenly
felt very cold and went up into the light.

IN THE ROME EXPRESS

T HE BLUE sleeping-cars of the Rome–Paris–
London express slip out of the terminus at
Rome shortly after 1 p.m. in an atmosphere
singularly free from interest. No one tries to
sell oranges to such a distinguished train. The
porters raise their caps as it moves off.

A steward immediately passes along the springy,
overheated corridors ringing a bell which announces luncheon. Men and their wives, men
by themselves, and solitary women—who never
appear more interesting and speculative than in
a *train de luxe*—pass along the chain of flying
dormitories to the opulent and alien display of
the restaurant car.

As the wine waiter lurches acrobatically round
with a bottle of branded Martinis, the engine,
emitting the toylike squeak peculiar to gigantic
Continental locomotives, picks up speed in open
country and pounds along at a good sixty miles
an hour.

A writer whose name I have forgotten chastised
his generation for ' dashing ' about Europe in
stage coaches. I look out of the window at the
Alban Hills which, owing to our speed, appear
to be performing a stately waltz, and wonder
what this man would have said to the peculiar
sight of a *train de luxe*.

In the old days when travel meant physical

hardship, men met together in an atmosphere of mutual respect. They compared notes of the perils that lay ahead. They were friends for the time being leagued against the elemental forces.

In a *train de luxe* we know that never, even by the wildest accident, shall we be forced to stand together as human beings against some monstrous peril—for we have paid our fares !—and therefore we sit, neat, washed and manicured, drinking wine and eating luncheon, moved only by a passing curiosity about each other.

There is the obvious King's Messenger with a Foreign Office bag, there is the man who wears mufti with a quarter-deck air on leave from Malta, there is the Italian business man going to Paris, and the Parisian business man returning from Rome, there is the inevitable American who may be a theatrical producer or the secretary of an embassy.

The mystery is the woman with carmine lips who toys delicately with her wineglass—lovely, thin fingers, and she knows it. She gazes at the men in turn as she might regard an insect stuck on a pin in a museum. There is something in her gaze which makes the men, with the exception of the Italians and perhaps the French, feel beautifully young and raw. The naval officer, who has been looking at destroyers for months, regards her furtively with an almost professional interest. The notable thing about her is that while her elegance is international, to every nationality present she appears foreign.

Who is she? Only the sleeping-car attendant knows, because he holds the passports. How interesting to be a sleeping-car attendant and to sit all night shuffling the credentials of international mysteries. She might be a great spy or a great actress or a great wife. It is impossible to say. She might even be one of those old-fashioned Oppenheimers who after the War were supposed to spend their lives tearing up and down the Corniche road in high-powered cars and an atmosphere of high politics.

Now that we mention it, she does look like that! Perhaps international intrigue is not so old-fashioned as we think. One touch with a cold, pale finger and a crown would topple and fall. Perhaps she is that strangest of all women—a morganatic wife. . . .

So as we fly across Europe she has the undivided attention of every man present, even of the husband who sits with his back to her. She knows this, and it braces her nerves.

The lovely Tuscan landscape flies past—hill towns lifted high above the plain, isolated farms, where women in bunchy skirts draw water from primitive wells; where queer cone-shaped haystacks, cut in long slices like cake, stand in rick yards; where palm trees grow queerly side by side with evergreens. There are towns of khaki-coloured houses with red-ribbed roofs, long, low and very Roman. The green shutters are fastened tight even in the depth of winter from force of habit. There is a flare of silver olive yards.

Dusk falls over the Tuscan plain. On the left the Tyrrhenian Sea gleams coldly, breaking silently on the rocks. We draw into a long, bleak station. Where are we? There is no visible name. Opposite in yellow lamplight are the offices : ' Ufficio Postale (Pacchi) ', ' Commando Militaire ', and ' Commando di Stazione '. Round them are the two insistent advertisers of Italy, ' Olio Sasso ' and ' Cinzano '.

' Where are we ? ' the mysterious woman is asking in French ! How hateful—how humiliating—not to know ! As stupid as a knight-errant who, when appealed to for help, had to say, ' I'm awfully sorry, but, you know, I've left my sword at home. . . .'

' Do you know where we are ? '

' I'm so sorry. . . .'

Down the bleak platform comes a small boy bearing a tray over his shoulders from which he holds something towards those who lean against the brass rail of the corridors, gazing up with big, hopeless eyes. He comes to me, and from the darkness of his tray lifts two objects which I think are small white candles. . . .

' Of course, of course ! Madame ! We are at Pisa ! '

And the wretched boy goes down the train on a task as hopeless as that of the man who tries to sell you a rug in Monte Carlo, holding up his little china leaning towers.

The train is asleep, or trying to sleep. We are speeding to the Alps in warmth and on springs

167

designed to save the nerves of the rich from unnecessary pain. Still we grumble ! It is so tiresome ! How on earth did Caesar get to Britain ? What appalling epics of travel were performed in ancient times. Think of the Punic elephants which the Emperor Claudius took with him to Colchester all the way from Rome. . . . Is the woman with the blood-red lips asleep on the special silken pillow which no doubt she carries round the world ? Suppose there was an accident, would the people lying prone in the hot, blue cars become real, or would we still remain strangers ? Only the brink of death, no doubt, would shake us from our reserve.

Outside in the corridor the car attendant sits sadly, his chocolate coat off and his cap tilted.

' It's no life for a man. I was married last week, and I see my wife only once in four days ! Then off again to Syracuse ! '

' What were you before you became a car attendant ? '

' I was in the Foreign Legion.'

Heavens, some people are never content !

To bed in the mystery of the *train de luxe*—a bed made by the comrade of Beau Geste—and in the grey dawn is a bump such as can be delivered only by an alien engine ; and the train is still for a long time.

Men stand outside in three feet of snow.

' What's the matter ? '

' The engine is frozen ! '

All round tower the frosted Alps.

168

'You have beautiful wedding cakes!'

The car attendant growls and curses the Alps under his breath. On the next track is another *train de luxe* going to Rome. There is a quick meeting of cooks, waiters and car attendants. Questions are asked, messages are given. Amazing meetings in the Alps when train passes train! A man from the train that left Paris yesterday comes jumping through the snow with a letter which the car attendant presses to his heart. It is from his beloved! It bears her latest kisses! It welcomes him home! He curses the frozen engine. We shall be late in Paris!

What a life!

The shades of night are falling as we crawl into the Gare de Lyons twelve hours late. The mystery of the carmine lips—more mysterious at lunch, desperately mysterious at dinner—waits in the corridor furred to the eyes. The train slides to a standstill, and the blue porters advance on it. The mysterious woman descends and falls with a sob into the arms of a fat and repulsive-looking man who, hat and cigar in one hand, presses her to his bosom crying:

'Darling!'

So she remains a deeper mystery than ever.

DESERT SANDS

SOME YEARS ago a woman wrote a novel that gave a new word to the English language —sheik. It crossed the Atlantic to return frequently in celluloid. A sheik is a determined and violent lover, and his original home is Algeria.

When you go to the desert you discover two things. First, do not call them 'sheeks'. They hate it. The real pronunciation is 'Shay-eek', but they don't mind if you make it 'shake'. Secondly, sheiks are of two kinds : home and colonial. The home kind are merely dull and the colonial variety is invisible. The town sheik wears pince-nez, reads Anatole France, receives a salary and a signed picture of the President from the French Government, lives in a kind of French villa that smells of rugs and stale coffee, and in the evening he plays 'I Aint Nobody's Darling' on a Pathéphone. I put it to you that this is not the real thing. This kind of sheik could be made French master in any girls' school with perfect safety.

So I set off early one morning to find the genuine Bad Boy of the Desert. And I set out on Ferdinand the Fiery. He was a typical desert steed—that is to say, he was mangy, old, knock-kneed and docile ; but, like some of the world's most antique motor-cars, he surprisingly worked.

When first I saw Ferdinand the Fiery I thought some one was pulling my leg. All Arab steeds wear blinkers, because they are liable (from constant galloping like streaks of lightning over the Sahara) to rather bad attacks of vertigo. His Roman nose reassured me. They always mean speed. All the same, I have never met any one to whom I desired more keenly to stand a bottle of champagne.

For one long day Ferdinand and I went on over the Sahara with the sun on us, till a sense of depression, striking upwards from the saddle, settled over my brain like a cloud. I have ridden horses of all kinds, have felt them wicked under me, have felt them good, have felt them wilful and even humorous. But Ferdinand was depressed. It was not the philosophic depression of a riding-school horse ; he seemed to be suffering from a recent bereavement. I dismounted many times, untied the string that held up his blinkers, and took a good look at his face. It then dawned on me that I was riding a haunted horse !

The next day before dawn I struck camp, watched the camels go off with the tent and the spirit stove, and once more sat down on Ferdinand.

What was haunting him ? I don't know. All I can tell is that the yellow waves of the desert seemed to hide a ghost. Although I knew there was no living thing in sight, I kept turning uneasily in the saddle . . . watching. It was rather horrible.

Then I began to wonder how on earth these sheiks manage to elope on their Ferdinands. I pictured the kind of luck I should have. Clutching the red-haired heroine to the saddle bow, I would say :

'And now, my sweet, forget the past and its sorrows. Let us fly ; and under a desert moon we will . . .'

'Yes, yes, I know,' she would say peevishly, 'but *do* start ! Arthur was shaving when I came down, and he'll be here in a minute.'

Then, closing my legs on Ferdinand and administering my heels, I would say, just to keep things moving :

'Never fear, little girl. In an hour we shall be miles away, the new life stretching out before us, the thunder of hoofs about us—just you and me.'

At this point I imagine the husband would come out of the hotel smoking a cigar, would walk after us, and hit Ferdinand with a stick, crying 'Gee up ! '

While I was thinking this I met my first real sheik.

'Bon jour, monsieur,' he said. He was a big, handsome fellow, in a travel-stained burnous. His eyes devoured Ferdinand. I felt that I ought to apologize.

'That is a fine horse ! ' he said.

Curse this Eastern politeness, I thought.

'Yes, first class,' I replied.

He invited me to his camp, a huddle of dirty

tents pitched out of the wind's way in a sand
hollow. There was a smell of garlic and high
game.

We took coffee. We talked. I discovered that
he had never abducted any one. That he didn't
want to. Romance bored him. He hated red
hair—the devil's colour. What really appealed
to him were chickens, dates and horses. Then
he got sheikish. I knew dirty work was coming. Would I exchange Ferdinand? My heart
thumped. He would give a beautiful horse in
return. My heart thundered. This was business
of the biggest kind. 'Show me!' I cried,
beginning to like him tremendously.

Outside, all ready for the deal, was something
that looked like Ferdinand's elder brother after
a terrible illness. A woman's voice called 'Ach-
med!' and the sheik, pulling himself together,
dashed like a rabbit round the tent. I ran in
for my hat.

When I came out the sheik was dominated by
an enormous woman in white plus twenty-fours
and a yashmak. She was alternately pointing
to the horses and hitting the palm of one hand
with the back of the other. At every sentence
her voice rose. The sheik wilted. He placed a
peaceful hand on her colossal arm. She shook
it off. He then kept repeating the Arabic for
'Yes, my love', and 'All right, my dear', and
'If you say so, my darling', till, with a jingle of
anklets, the monumental woman turned and
concealed herself under canvas. The sheik came

back to me apologetically. He looked at the horses :

'The Moon of my Delight forbids,' he said simply. We shook hands, and I rode off with new ideas on sheiking.

That night was the night of the full moon. I was sitting at the tent-flap smoking, wondering if it would be worth while to bring out a real horse, also an outfit from Clarkson, and start a school for sheiks under the presidentship of women novelists. Suddenly something about Ferdinand made me sit up ! He was standing picketed in a patch of green light, head thrust forward, silent, still. Behind him, for a brief second, clear as if outlined in phosphorescent paint, I saw a ghostly cab.

Whether it was imagination or whether he is haunted by one of his past lives I really do not know.

THE OUTCAST

SOME WELL-MEANING friend had given me a
letter of introduction to a Mr. Snap of Cairo.
It is very difficult to travel without such things.
I had no intention of using it and, in fact, in-
tended to destroy it. It seemed rather grotesque
to meet a Mr. Snap in Cairo, and in any case
he sounded the slick kind of business man that
I loathe.

I was sitting one day on that famous but
absurd terrace of Shepheards Hotel which, more
than any other place I know, creates the illusion
that one is taking part in a musical comedy.
White-hot sunlight blazed down. The palm-
leaves had stopped rasping. Even the warm
wind had died away.

American girls sat at the hot little tables,
accompanied by their prematurely withered
mothers and their sallow good-natured fathers.
A snake-charmer was chanting to a doped cobra
for the embarrassed benefit of a middle-aged
English couple who did not want to see the
snake but had not been sufficiently long in Egypt
to possess the correct formula for driving off the
importunate. Dragomans with the boldest eyes
and the filthiest minds in the world gazed brazenly
at the scene in search of prey. They are not
allowed to ascend the steps, but they stand on
them. Beyond the rails the crazy muddle of

Cairene life went by in the street. A native
prince whom I recognized as a harmless ass
whom even the Cavalry School, during the War,
could not teach to sit a horse (I think he used
to say his legs were the wrong shape) sat at
the wheel of a big red Hispano-Suiza. I remember how drunk we made him on Guinness
and Benedictine the night before they passed
him for political reasons into the Household
Cavalry. Now, looking fat and dissipated, he
sat at the wheel of his great car, waiting for
a line of tattered camels loaded with *bersim* to
give way to him. A water-carrier with goat-
skin over his shoulder banged brass cups together
as he went shouting down the street. A veiled
woman passed wearing gold anklets over silk
stockings. A posse of Egyptian mounted police
came along, little red and white flags fluttering
from their lances. Victorias clip-clopped through
the crowd, large pock-marked guides sitting beside the driver and turning every now and then
to explain something with a strong American
accent.

Through the rails that separated the rich ones,
or the apparently rich ones, of this earth from
the vulgar streets, were thrust lean brown arms
terminating in thin hands bearing post cards.
Some of the post cards were violently coloured
views of the pyramids ; others exhibited large
and undulate women in a state of unpleasant
nudity. Becoming weary of offering these cards,
the owners would grope in the folds of their

galabiyehs and suddenly thrust forward a handful of spurious scarabs or a string of doubtful mummy beads. It was at this moment that Mr. Snap was announced.

I saw a strange little old man making his way to me between the tables. He wore a panama hat, blue sun spectacles and a grey flannel suit. He bowed stiffly in a formal foreign way and told me, with a slight alien accent, that our mutual friend in England had written telling him of my arrival, so he had taken the liberty of calling before I presented the letter of introduction. My first impression was that he had been eating garlic.

There was about him that air of putting the best face on things which becomes so pitiful when assumed by middle-aged women who apply for minor secretarial posts in offices. He had, in other words, spruced himself up. I knew instinctively that he was not normally like this. I wondered why he had made this effort.

We sat down and I asked him to have a drink. He made such a show of refusal, saying that it was too early or too late or not his normal habit, that I thought to myself : ' This man is a drunkard and is pretending to be abstemious '. In the end he rather too eagerly drank a large whisky.

The negative personality of little Mr. Snap began to interest me. It was too hot to do much active speculation, so I just sat watching him, thinking what strange characters are torn from

their context and flung into odd parts of the
earth. But what had been his context ? He had
watery blue eyes and an eruptive nose. It looked
as though some skin disease had never been
properly cured.

He was really remarkably shabby, but somehow did not seem so until you examined him in
detail. I noticed that his extremities were perfect. His brown shoes were good and new as
though they were treed up every night, and his
hands were well cared for. He had small hands
and feet. Yet there was something weak and
shifty and—how can I explain it ?—*déclassé* about
him. I felt sure he was a good old man, but I
had the suspicion that he might have been a bad
young one.

When the whisky worked in him he lost his
uncertain, ill-at-ease air and became rather
talkative. I discovered that he was a scholar.
He began to talk familiarly about the Pharaonic
dynasties, frequently quoting Herodotus in Greek
or putting in a sentence from Strabo or Plutarch,
but never with the affectation of the consciously
learned. It was strange to hear this queer little
old man worshipping the distant past in his
foreign voice. He said that he would like to
show me something of Egypt, and, suddenly
gathering up his panama hat and a pair of brown
kid gloves, shook hands and departed.

I awakened in the night and wondered about
Mr. Snap, that strange little old man. I sat at
my window high up at the back of Shepheards,

level with the ostrich plumes of the palm-trees, and I looked down on the red sand of the garden listening to the steady thud of distant drums, wondering how this little Englishman with his alien accent and his haunting suggestion of garlic came to be lost in Africa.

I could not decide whether I liked or disliked him, which for me is an unusual and disturbing condition. I usually know as soon as I set eyes on a man. But Mr. Snap was different.

In the morning he called again. He said that he just happened to be passing. I took him into the bar and, without asking for his permission, gave him a large drink. He took off his panama hat and placed it neatly on the marble ledge of the bar, his kid gloves precisely laid beside it. This time he talked not of Pharaohs but of England :

' Bai Jove,' he said, ' I suppose London's altered a lot since my time. Yes, bai Jove . . .'

I wondered when ' his time ' might have been, but I was still more interested in the ' bai Jove '. I was listening to the accent of a Piccadilly ' masher ' of 1870.

' When were you last in London ? ' I asked.

' Oh, bai Jove,' he replied, laughing wickedly, ' it must be at least six . . . no ; fifty years ago. I remember that Disraeli was Prime Minister, yes, bai Jove.'

The strangest things flow from one person to

another, things of which both may be unconscious. I knew that this old man wanted to be
talked to as if he were my contemporary. I regarded him as a curiosity. The snob in me disliked being seen with him, because in the sunlight he had a frayed and disreputable look.
But I suddenly warmed to him. There was
something about him terribly real and pitiful.
Women married to drunkards must feel like this.
I wanted to help him, I wished he would have
asked me to 'lend' him ten pounds. I liked
something that was buried deeply in him, far
beyond the possibility of excavation. Perhaps
a man of my own age and upbringing was
speaking to me from the Piccadilly of 1870. It
was very odd.

'Bai Jove,' he said suddenly, 'I wonder if you
know the Snaps of Lincolnshire?'

'I'm afraid I don't.'

'One of the oldest families in England,' he
said simply.

'Giles de Snape was at the battle of Hastings.'

'Really,' I said in an absurd tone of voice.

'Oh yes, bai Jove,' said Mr. Snap, taking a
long drink, 'and another Snap helped to draw
up Magna Charta. Of course you've heard of
the Sir Charles Snap who held Ruxmore Castle
against the Cromwellians?'

'Oh; that Snap,' I said.

Mr. Snap put down his glass and faced me
solemnly.

'Yes,' he said. 'Oh, bai Jove, yes.'

He said again that he would dearly like to show Egypt to me and went away, leaving me wondering whether he would show me something obscene in the Fish Market or the chaste dignity of the Boulak Museum.

I began to understand Mr. Snap very well ; but fortunately he did not know this. He began to call every day. Sometimes I was in, sometimes I was out. Often he would come up to my room and sit on the edge of the bed while I finished dressing, saying ' bai Jove ' and ' how fraightfully good ' until I began to feel that something had escaped from Gilbert and Sullivan. I have never met anything, except perhaps the Crystal Palace, quite so mid-Victorian as Mr. Snap.

We became more friendly day after day. He was always penniless. He adored to sit back with a big cigar, after a good luncheon or dinner in Shepheards or the Continental Savoy, but he always shuddered with the horror of one who has known poverty when the extortionate bill came round. He felt happy and at home, but he always saw the money which paid for his happiness as something which could have been more wisely expended.

He liked me—it seems a funny thing to say of a red-nosed old man who smelt of garlic—because I appealed to his better self. I liked him because it amused me to watch his inherent good breeding coming out. I suppose I had never met a submerged gentleman before, or at least I had never met a harmless one before. He had a good effect on me too. I became more considerate and punctilious. I was translated by his idea of me into an age of better manners. There were moments during our talks about the London of 1870 and the Snaps of Lincolnshire when I would not have been surprised to see Queen Victoria enter the room leaning on the arm of Albert the Good. And the very lovely American girl might have been surprised to know that I evaded her dance at the Gezira Palace because I was more interested in old Snap and had promised to dine with him.

He took me to some ghastly native restaurant where they served a series of hellish hors-d'œuvres on little plates, all of which tasted bad and sour. But we had a good time. (After dark, little Snap in his frayed flannel suit always seemed to be in full evening dress.) It was on this occasion that he, under the influence of some particularly foul wine, told me that his nose was red because a dog had once bitten it. I remember thinking that he had been taking a hair of this dog ever since. When the bill came round I had a violent desire to pay it, but had I done so I knew that Snap would never have seen me again. I watched him bring out a little leather purse and painfully count out piastres.

Although I understood that he was a submerged English gentleman who responded to my accept-ance of him as such, I could never visualize his background. I could see him more clearly against the Strand of 1870 than in modern Cairo.

Where did he go when I said : ' Well, good-
night, Snap. See you to-morrow ' ? Where did
he go ? Into what mystery did he fade with
his rather tipsy—the right old Victorian word—
jauntiness and his panama hat ? I thought he
was a bachelor until one night, apologizing for
something, he said that he would so much like
me to dine at home with him only, alas, his wife
was unwell.

We went out to Giza and looked at the pyramids and the Sphinx. I hired two quite good
horses and he rode one of them with an air,
saying that he would be very sore in the morning, but looking like some one that Velasquez
might have painted. In spite of his dog-bitten
nose, old Snap was an aristocrat. Spineless and
drunken he might be, but what an excellent
king he would have made. His gentleness would
have been taken for condescension, his furtive
ingenuousness for simplicity.

And in the moonlight at Giza he made the
past of Egypt alive. His foreign voice rose in
faint breaths of garlic, re-building the past so
clearly that I sat in a kind of enchantment. He
was a pure classicist. Everything that had happened since the fall of Rome was barbarianism.
He much preferred to talk in Greek or Latin.
That was his world. Sitting his horse in the
moonlight, he became, in some vague way,
splendid and heroic as he re-created the vanished
centuries, sending old chariots thundering across
the world.

'Did I tell you,' he said as we rode back over the straight road to Cairo, 'that I wrote the standard biography on Hatshepsut? What a woman! Nobody bought it, but I sometimes get second-hand book catalogues in which it is quoted at three guineas. It seems wrong that I should never have made three guineas out of it, doesn't it? Bai Jove, what a woman . . .'

I think Mr. Snap's peculiarities must have hypnotized me. Day after day I went about with him, trying to cap his quotations from Horace and Juvenal. I wondered very often how he could afford to give so much time to me; and this worried me. If only a punctilious gentleman had not been mummified somewhere inside him I might have asked him to accept a shameful fiver with my gratitude. But not Snap. It simply could not happen. Much as he needed and desired the money, I could not offer it to him. I had not the courage or the necessary insensitiveness. And you had only to see Snap sitting up on a high stool at an American bar, revelling in his return to leisure and expensive hotels, to realize how impossible was this.

One night I dined in the Turf Club. A man I knew slightly said:

'I saw you the other day with that old ruffian Snap. I should be a bit careful if I were you. Has he touched you yet?'

I was rather curt and on the defensive. I stood up for Snap. I liked him. But I was curious about him. I tried not to ask questions about my strange little old friend :

'This is the trouble, of course,' said the man, pretending to drain a glass. 'Queer fellow, but clever. Oh ; before he ran on the rocks he was something in the consular service. Drank himself out of it. There was some romantic story. An American girl. She let him down. That was years ago before we were born. What does he do now ? No one knows. He's gone right down. Lives in some awful native quarter. He married a low-class Greek girl. I believe she was a laundress or something like that. One simply can't be seen with him. I mean we can't. It's all right for you : you don't live here. . . .'

So that was the mystery of Snap, the little English gentleman who had submerged himself with a Greek laundress. It was probably some mistaken loyalty to Sophocles.

'He's smartened up considerably since you took him up,' went on my friend, 'but he'll crash as soon as you move on, poor old devil.'

And the time came when I did move on. Snap arrived, faithful to the last, shabby but well shod and gloved. He smelt abominably of garlic, a smell which suggested to me oily and repulsive meals prepared by the Greek girl. I felt un-utterably sorry for him. He looked so small and lost standing on the station platform :

'Bai Jove, I'm sorry you're going,' he said, hitting his leg with the kid gloves that he carried. It was a dashing little gesture. I suppose they did it in Piccadilly in the 'seventies.

Just before the train moved out an expression of deep concern passed over his face. He dived into his pocket and appeared dismayed :

'Bai Jove,' he said, 'I've left all my money at home. I've got to take a taxi. I wonder— I wonder if you could lend me ten piastres.'

Ten piastres. Poor little Snap. I pretended that I had no change and gave him a hundred piastre note. He dived off to the booking-office and returned with ninety piastres which he handed to me. Ten, he assured me, was quite enough for his taxi. The train moved off and the last thing I saw was the waving of a large panama hat.

Months afterwards, when I had forgotten all about Mr. Snap, a stilted formal letter arrived, sprinkled with tags and quotations, and the burden of the letter was that times were not too good and would I forget about the ten piastres and accept a book instead ? When I undid the parcel a large book was revealed entitled : *The Queen Hatshepsut, her Life and Times.*

It was obviously his own copy, his one link with a world from which he had receded. And as I turned the exceedingly learned pages his gift seemed to me a supreme, pitiful gesture of farewell.

UP THE NILE

THE FINEST selection of tourists in the world is to be discovered at Luxor. They arrive in successive droves, dash over to Karnak, run round Luxor Temple, rush over to the Valley of the Tombs, and then depart in the direction of Assuan, leaving an impression behind as of nothing accomplished, nothing done.

Who are they, and why do they do this? A native told me that Allah sent them so that men might live. The fatality of the East must have got into my blood, for I really believe this is the only explanation.

It is early morning in Luxor. The Nile lies like a sheet of pearl, so still that you feel you could walk over the water to the other bank, where the pink hills of the Valley of the Tombs rise up, changing colour as the sun rides the sky. Feluccas like big white moths are skimming over the river, full of men in baseball knickers and sweaters and girls wearing riding-breeches and silk stockings.

On the opposite bank a solid phalanx of donkeys and donkey-boys runs at them. Eventually they mount and ride away over mudflats planted with water-melon, between fields of tall sugar-cane, through a mud village in a palm grove, which might have stepped out of Genesis, and up to the tawny mouth of the Valley of the Tombs, where the heat comes out at them like a wave.

On and on they ride, twisting this way and that as the little rock path goes up into the heart of the valley. A kite hovers in the navy-blue sky, a lizard flashes from a hot stone like a green streak.

' So this is the darned old Valley of the Dead. Guess they might have put it a bit nearer civilization.'

' If you please, gentlemans, we will now visit the tomb of Rameses the Fourth.'

The dragoman in his purple *abayeh* smiles and leads the way into the cool darkness of the grave.

A few moments later the indomitable band may be seen climbing over the Theban Hills towards Der el Bahari. Up they go over the gold rocks right in the eye of the sun, and down they dip on the other side of the valley, where Queen Hatshepsut's temple is cut so beautifully in the side of the hill.

In the blaze of afternoon on they go to the Ramesseum. Half an hour afterwards they ride off towards the temple of Medinet Habu, one of the most beautiful things in the whole world. Towards tea-time the Colossi, sitting on the edge of a green plain like Darby and Joan beside the fire, look down to see the inexhaustible cavalcade halted at their feet.

How tired the Colossi must be of it all ! They have been receiving tourists since the time of Herodotus.

It is night. An afterglow of pink, fading to yellow and mother-of-pearl, has given way to a blue sky of stars. The new moon, holding the pale ghost of the old moon in its horns, sails the night and cuts a path of rippling light across the Nile. On the far bank a native boy with a flute is playing a few chords which Verdi stole and introduced most beautifully in 'O Terra Addio' in *Aïda*. And over Egypt lies an unspeakable sadness, a feeling of something lost and crying, for ever uncomforted and inconsolable, in the beauty of the night.

The hotel lounge is dotted with exhausted damsels and weary swains. They write in little morocco-bound books and look up pathetically, pencil at lip.

'Say, Gus, what did we do second day?'

'Darned if I know. Put down Ramesseum!'

'Gus.'

'Yes?'

'What was the name of that place with the big statue?'

'Oh, some kind of god house. I've forgotten, kid.'

'Gus.'

'Yes?'

'Got your notes on Jerusalem there?'

'Yes.'

'Am I right in telling momma that we "did" the Church of the Holy Sepulchre?'

'Risk it.'

'Gus.'

'Yes?'

'What was the name of that dragoman with the big eyes?'

I wonder what happens to these congested records of rush. Perhaps some day an editor will discover in one the soul of Egypt.

I love to think so.

THE PYRAMID BUILDERS

ONE EVENING at sunset I sat in the warm sand at the foot of the Sphinx and watched small birds make love to him. They flew round in sweeping circles as if they hoped to win a smile. The sun dropped below the desert. The three great Pyramids were black against rose colour, then black against a lemon-coloured sky, and finally, stark and mountainous, lifting themselves to the blue mantle of the night.

Sitting there in the silence I saw the Sphinx awaken and come to life. His hollow eyes filled, and round his full lips played a smile, in which I read all the hunger and perplexity and all the faith that lives in the heart of man. And I thought that he who made the Sphinx, whoever he was, was one of the greatest men the world has ever known.

Who were these men and what were they like, these far-distant workers in the very dawn of the world? They are so far off, just shadows moving in a mist of time, ghostly, unknown people. Suddenly an American archaeologist digging in Egypt enters a dark cavern that has been shut from the eyes of men for four thousand five hundred years, and lo, a curtain seems to shake a little, to lift slightly on history, and we peer through into the fog where the dim figures of that time move across the stage of life. What do we see?

The drama of humanity has begun. In the Nile Valley the first great cities of the world are thronged with life. Thousands of years of un-recorded struggle have led to an organized society centred round the temple and the palace. The rest of the world is sunk in barbarism, but on the Nile float garlanded ships in which women listen to the first love songs, across the deserts troops advance to war, over the seas of the early world the first argosies go in search of wonder and profit ; and in his palace at Memphis the most powerful man of that time, the Pharaoh of Egypt, Snefru, dreams of forming the first great commercial kingdom.

He mines copper in Sinai, he sends his sailors to Lebanon for wood to beautify his palace, he brings gold from the Sudan, so that all the wealth of the virgin world pours into the treasuries of Egypt, and thus the foundations of the first empire have been laid.

Then come a line of men who might have been blotted from human memory had not their fear of death and their belief in after-life caused them to erect the mighty monuments which have re-mained a mystery and a wonder ever since—the Pyramid Kings.

Cheops, Cephren, and Mykerinos are the three men who built the three great Pyramids four thousand years ago.

Why did they build them and how ? That is a question which later ages have always asked. ' If only Khufu (Cheops) had allowed his master architect to write a description of the building of the Great Pyramid, what a wonderful document it would be ! ' wrote Sir Ernest Wallis Budge. Wonderful ? It would be one of the most astonishing documents ever penned !

Here, in the beginning of history, one man's will was capable of directing other men to pile up for him an incredible tomb containing 2,300,000 blocks of quarried stone, each block of which weighed two and a half tons. That is Sir Flinders Petrie's estimate of the bulk of the Pyramid of Cheops. Herodotus repeats a tradition current in his time that the building of the Great Pyramid demanded the labour of 100,000 men for twenty years, and Petrie has shown that this is credible.

Round each Pyramid must have grown up a city, markets, and temples. Families must have been reared in the shadow of the slow-rising mass of stone. Men must have grown old and grey in the labour of cutting the stone, of dragging it to the site, of hauling, year after year, the great blocks up the inclined ramp of sand from which each stone was set in place. How much misery, how much blood, how many tears went to their building we can only guess, for you hear the whistle of a whip as the files of slaves bend their backs to the work.

Behind all this effort stands a marvellous unknown man—the architect. With no machinery but hard stones to bash out the rock from its bed, and nothing but human muscles to put the stones in place, he built this gigantic structure with so fine a finish that you have to run your finger-nail over the stone to find the joints. Blocks weighing tons are set, says Petrie, with a skill involving edges and surfaces 'equal to opticians' work of the present day '.

Then, vanity of vanities, when the great mass was finished, when the huge city was evacuated, the Pharaoh would no doubt look at his Pyramid, and feel happy in the pathetic belief that his body would lie safe in the dark depths of it, waiting secure from Time.

The Pyramids in their glory must have been one of the most amazing sights in the world. Here was a city of the dead. Round each pyramid rose the tombs of the nobles and the royal kinsmen. The Pharaoh's tomb lorded it over their humbler tombs as his palace rose above their houses, but as they lived side by side so in death they slept together on the fringe of the desert.

They enjoyed life as much as they respected death. The king's armies went out and returned victorious. Tribute and captives filled his cities. Wealth bred culture, art, elegance. One picture of Snefru has been preserved for us which is deathless. Twenty beautiful girls in dresses of transparent network rowed his Majesty in his royal barge, dipping paddles of ivory inlaid with gold into the blue waters of the Nile. One girl dropped her ring into the river, and, says the legend, the waters, at a word from the king's magician, divided, one portion standing upon the other portion, and below lay the ring with which Pharaoh soothed the tears of his handmaiden.

So, four thousand five hundred years ago, in this age of splendour and power, the foundations of the world's first empire were laid by men whose works are those of supermen, whose motives, so full of vanity and fear, link them to us in a common frailty over a great brink of Time.

ST. ANDREW'S SHRINE

THE YOUNG man descended on me with
indecent joy as I was drinking a flask of
white Orvieto. Vines made a green tunnel of
shade ; and beyond them the summer sun blazed
down on Amalfi.

'You wanta guide,' said the young man eagerly.
'Me good. Me speaka da English. Me know
all about Mr. Gladstone and Mr. Longfellow.'

I waved him off, but he returned with the
speed and determination of a mosquito. I pretended to look angry as I gazed sternly at the
lovely town below, lying on a slope of the
Apennines with a blue bay at its feet. Then I
made a fatal mistake. He said something which
caused me to smile.

'And I show you the tomb of Sant' Andrea,'
he said, seeing his advantage.

His brown eyes gleamed. He knew that he
had won me !

St. Andrea ? That is the Italian for St.
Andrew. Which St. Andrew was it ?

'Sant' Andrea,' said the young man, 'the
brother of Sant' Pietro. . . .'

Then it was St. Andrew, the Apostle, brother
of Simon Peter and the patron saint of Scotland,
who lies so far from the land of his adoption
above the blue bay of Amalfi.

We went down through the vines to the town.

The tall Saracenic houses trapped the shade. In the central square above a great flight of steps stood the Cathedral of St. Andrew. How many Scotsmen, I wonder, know the history of their saint? St. Andrew of Scotland (and Russia) was the first disciple to be called by Our Lord.

He was a fisherman of Bethsaida in Galilee. After the Crucifixion he travelled in Russia, Scythia and Greece, where he made converts. One of these converts was the wife of the Roman magistrate in Patrae, in the Peloponnesus. The husband, furious that his wife should have embraced the new religion, ordered the Apostle to be crucified. He was bound to the X-shaped cross that bears his name, and his agonies were great.

The body of St. Andrew was taken to Constantinople and interred beside the body of St. Luke. At some time before the ninth century certain relics of the saint, so legend says, found their way into Scotland, where they were reverently housed in the little grey town which became known as St. Andrews. For centuries the body of St. Andrew remained in Constantinople until Cardinal Pietro Capuano, a native of Amalfi, brought the saint's body as a precious gift to his town in the year 1208.

We went down into the dim crypt of the cathedral. Beneath an altar and in a blaze of tapers was a gold sarcophagus containing the remains of Scotland's saint. The young man knelt reverently before them and told me of the 'manna di Sant' Andrea '—a miraculous oily fluid which, so the Amalfians believe, exudes from the saint's bones once a year in November. He described how the Archbishop descends into the crypt with a glass phial. Sometimes the 'manna' comes in quantity, at others the phial is only damp with it.

This phenomenon is similar to that which is said to occur in many other Italian shrines when saintly blood liquefies once a year. The late Lord Bute obtained a small tube of St. Andrew's 'manna'.

'It looks just like water,' he wrote, 'and I have an impression that it could be accounted for by the condensation of moisture in this dark vault, often crowded with people ; and that some infrequency of such phenomena, or change of temperature, opening or shutting windows, etc., could explain the change. . . .'

But the people of Amalfi believe that St. Andrew chooses this method of communicating to them a loving interest in their well-being.

'When the manna comes,' said the young man, 'we have a very good year. Not much manna, not such a good year. . . .'

St. Andrew's town in Scotland is to-day more interested in golf than in holy relics, and Russia, which also claims St. Andrew as its patron saint, has perhaps forgotten him also. But Amalfi has built its spiritual life round the Apostle. All things good are attributed to his pleasure ; all things bad to his wrath.

'I always pray to St. Andrew,' said the young man. 'I find that he answers prayers quicker than the Virgin,' he added simply.

'And why is that?' I asked.

He then explained to me his theory that the prayers of Amalfi go straight to St. Andrew, whereas the Virgin, with a whole world's prayers to deal with, could not be expected to respond so promptly.

'And we proved it last year', continued the young man, 'when Amalfi was flooded. The waters poured down from the hills. We prayed to God; and it still rained! Then we prayed to the Virgin, but nothing happened. Then we came here and asked St. Andrew to stop the floods; and at once they were stopped.'

He knelt and crossed himself:

'I always come to St. Andrew,' he whispered.

There was something so businesslike about his attitude that I could not help feeling most Scotsmen would have sympathized with him.

So we left the dark crypt and the bones of the saint who gave his name to Scotland and helped to form the Union Jack. I tried to explain this to the devout young follower of St. Andrew, but it was very difficult—because he had never heard of Scotland!

THE BLUE ISLE

From my balcony in Capri the vineyards slope down to the sea and far off, beyond the horizon, is Sicily.

When night falls, sea and sky blend together in a deep, uniform blue. It is difficult to say which is sea and which is sky, because the sea also has its stars. They shine over miles of still blue water, little twinkling points of fire which move slowly as if forming experimental constellations. These are the fishermen of Capri who go out every night with lamps in their rowing-boats to catch the queer creatures that haunt the southern seas.

The other night I put on a pair of rope shoes and fisherman's trousers and went out with the Capri fleet. Old Salvatore, the fisherman, had beached his boat on the Marina Grande. The sun had set, but a pink flush filled the sky.

We pushed off over a sea like blue glass. Away to the east we saw Vesuvius, dark and sinister, his head plumed with sulphur-tinted smoke. The lights of Naples lay to our left like a string of jewels round the neck of the night.

Round us for miles shone the lamps of the Caprean boats ; and I was glad that the sea was smooth, because a frailer fleet cannot fish in any waters.

Old Salvatore is on the verge of seventy. He

goes barefoot and has the figure of a lad of
eighteen. He tells me as we row out to sea that
he is the father of fourteen children :
'Ten good,' he says, 'and four no good ! '
'I am sorry,' I said lamely, with painful
visions of idle or ungrateful sons.
'No good,' he repeats sadly, 'four dead, but
ten alive and—good ! '
How on earth do these men manage to establish
such large and thriving families ? Three sons, he
says, are in America and one in Paris.
'They must go away to make their fortunes,'
he explains.
There is something Elizabethan in the way
these fishermen's sons go to the Americas in
search of riches, dreaming always of returning to
settle down in Italy.
As we row to sea dusk falls over Capri. I
look back on steep hills rising blackly from the
sea as if cut in velvet against the sky. The Milky
Way lies above us like a veil of thin gauze. A
new moon hangs in the sky. There is no sound
but the creak of our little boat, the cool splash
of our oars in the warm sea and the voice of
Salvatore, high-pitched and aged, singing *Bella
Capri*.
No wonder the fishermen of Capri sing a love-
song to their island every night when they go
out to earn their living by lamplight.
We took a canful of water and carbide and,
setting it on the gunwale of the boat, lit a lamp
that sent a pool of light eddying around us.

' It is ', said Salvatore, fumbling badly for English words and ending amusingly in French, ' *très intéressant pour les poissons.*'

I cannot help smiling as I fling in a villainous spinning-bait to ' interest ' the poor fish of the Gulf of Salerno !

Now any one who has visited the Naples Aquarium must fish these waters with some apprehension. What would I catch ? An octopus ? A great coloured head with human eyes ? A fairy fish or some snapping, shark-like horror ?

Nothing happened ! Salvatore began to sing a plaintive invocation to Neptune. I watched his fine old head bent earnestly over his line in the light of the acetylene jet. Suddenly that international expression—the joy of a man who has hooked a fish—came over his face, and he began rapidly to haul in his line.

What had he caught ? I looked astern, where something wild was thrashing the water, something luminous and strange. He pulled it in, and held up in the light of our lamp a little mad rainbow ! It was a fish about six inches long and shaped like a torpedo. Its head was horrible, the head of a magnified shrimp to which were attached the tentacles of an octopus. These waved in the air and attempted to grip the boat. But the body of this strange thing was like pink and silver celluloid, with patches of blue and gold and green in it. It was iridescent with colour.

' Tortoni,' said Salvatore, ' good to eat.'

To my horror he took it from the hook and flung it over to me. The thing lay beside me, thrusting out its tentacles. When I bent down to see it better, it gave two extremely alarming sneezes. It was a calamaro or ink-fish, called by the Capreans 'tortoni'.

There is nothing more monotonous than good fishing—except perhaps bad fishing. To pull trout after trout out of a burn is indescribably tedious, and to encounter a shoal of whiting or mackerel is even more boring.

Fishing for tortoni by lamplight is like this. The mad rainbows follow the light; they dash recklessly at the absurd bait; and you sit there hour after hour reluctantly detaching the creatures from the hooks.

We sang *O Sole Mio*; and even this did not deter the tortoni from rushing on death. No two fishes were the same colour. We pulled in white, blue, silver, gold, red, green and variegated tortoni until the bottom of the boat was a pile of prismatic limpness. In one thing only were they alike—their habit of sneezing unexpectedly when lifted from the water.

'Nothing but tortoni to-night,' said Salvatore, 'the sea is too smooth. Far out, perhaps, they catch sword-fish.'

'How long do these fishermen stay out?'

'All night,' said Salvatore. 'Then they sleep all day while the women sell the fish in the market.'

We crossed the bows of another boat and heard

the men singing as they pulled in their lines. I thought of sterner fishing in Aberdeen and Grimsby and Milford Haven, where men sing no songs as they go out in the drive of northern waters.

When the moon had sunk we landed by star-light on a little deserted beach. The water was warm as we waded in to pull up the boat. Far away, in the Gulf of Salerno, we saw the lights, like fallen stars, still riding the sea.

VICTORIA

N OTHING IS quite so flattering to self-esteem
or so fatal to a sense of internationalism
as the act of entering a Pullman car at Dover.
You have been away for a long time in foreign
places, eating foreign foods, spending unreal-
looking money, suffering the indignity of customs
and the cynical suspicion of passport officers, and
then the boat slides into the calm waters of Dover
Harbour and the English porters run aboard.
You are home again.

Returning home is an emotion which can be
overrated. It is sometimes more joyful to contemplate arrival than to arrive, because home is
frequently never more appealing than when you
are not there. It is difficult to know, in all the
emotions of life, how much we contribute to the
object sentimentalized from the rich store of our
own imaginations. Men who do vaguely worth-
while things in colonies and return sunburnt after
many years to wander miserably about London
until their leave is up, experience in an acute
form the sharp conflict that separates the real
from the ideal. Home is not what it once was,
and the cynic might say that perhaps it never
was.

This does not, however, apply to Dover and
the train that goes to Victoria. Here we enter
an ideal world, secure for two hours or so from

the resounding impact of reality. If there is any
love of country in a man, how it rises in his
heart when he meets again the well-ordered
routine of English life, the hearty voices of the
porters, the flattering recognition of the Pullman
attendant ; and how proud is any man to belong
to a country which has no need to chain nail-
brushes to a lavatory basin. When you come
from lands whose sanitary arrangements seem to
be the inspiration of demented or humorous
plumbers, how good it is to be in England, where
everything works.

The train rushes through interminable suburbs
and at length crosses the jewelled Thames. You
do not remember with what joy you left London
a few months earlier, with what relief you cast
yourself in the corner of a carriage and declined
to look out and see the last of Victoria as the
train steamed off. You know only that you are
home and that the lights of London look brighter
and more significant than the lights of any other
city in the world. You approach Paris with excitement ; you approach London with happiness.
Everything about London looks so reliable, so
proofed in sanity. The crowds rushing home to
Beckenham seem composed entirely of splendid
men and beautiful women. You begin to see
your absence almost in the light of treachery.
There is something friendly and inexplicably
comforting even in the dull acquiescence of the
taxi-driver. A good fellow, a typical Londoner !

This exaltation, which is the feeling of belonging to something, may last a day or perhaps two. But while it lasts it is a good, warm feeling. If there is ever another war, and if the publicity men fill the ranks with posters about England, Home and Beauty, I shall sit in my trench and, performing the difficult task of enumerating those things for which I am fighting, set down among them the platform at Dover Harbour and the Pullman attendant who seldom forgets my name.

NOTE

Some of these essays originally appeared in the *Daily Herald*, the *Daily Express* and the *Sunday Express*, but many of them are printed here for the first time.

Printed in Great Britain by Butler & Tanner Ltd., Frome and London

THE 'SEARCH' BOOKS

A BOOK by H. V. Morton is more than a travel book: it is a sensitive interpretation of a country's people and their history. The success, five years ago, of his first book on England, established the popularity of something new and refreshing in this type of literature. Since that time Mr. Morton's gay and informative travels through Scotland, Ireland and Wales have gained him thousands of readers in all parts of the world.

The 'Search' books have been called the ideal gift books, and they are recognized as the perfect companions for a tour of the various countries which they describe.

The author has frequently been requested to define the secret of writing a travel book. He always replies : ' There is no secret. You either enjoy yourself or you do not. If you do, say so ; if you do not—say so ! '

This disarming sincerity is, perhaps, responsible for the charm and fascination of his books. The feel and smell of the countryside, also a sense of movement, find their way into these light-hearted wanderings, and, combined with humour, acute observation, sympathy and an engaging curiosity, have justly gained for them a wide and increasing popularity.

IN SEARCH OF WALES

With 16 Illustrations and a Map. 7s. 6d. net

The Right Hon. DAVID LLOYD GEORGE, reviewing ' In Search of Wales ' in the *Daily Herald*, calls it :—

' The best travel book on Wales that I have ever read. . . . If there were a crown for the most distinguished stranger of the year at the next Eisteddfod, I would back MORTON. And I would set the crown firmly on his brow with my own hands.'

' Anyone who has enjoyed one or all of the earlier volumes will not be long separated from the fourth.'—*British Weekly*.

' What a charmer Mr. H. V. MORTON is ! . . . He is a great ambassador, and this book of his should do for Wales what his previous books have done for Ireland and Scotland.'—*Morning Post*.

' He has made the guide-book a vehicle of literature.'—*Sphere*.

' One of the most interesting books, both descriptive and historical, that has been written about Wales.'—*North Wales Weekly News*.

IN SEARCH OF ENGLAND

With 18 Illustrations and a Map. 7s. 6d. net

' If you ask me to name the perfect summer book, I reply without hesitation, " In Search of England." . . . He is a modern COBBETT, and this rich book is for us more readable than " Rural Rides ".'—*Sunday Express*.

' Mr. H. V. MORTON exhibits something of a Borrovian charm in his narrative of personal adventure.'—*Manchester Guardian*.

' Everything he touches turns to a story under his hand ; he fills his pages with life and character.'—*The Bookman*.

THE CALL OF ENGLAND

With 16 Illustrations and a Map. 7s. 6d. net

' If one's holiday is over, here are ideas for the next ; if one's holiday is to come, here is a place that must be seen ; if there can be no holiday at all, here is a good substitute.'—*The Bookman*.

' A truly enchanting book.'—*The Tatler*.

IN SEARCH OF SCOTLAND

With 16 Illustrations and a Map. 7s. 6d. net

Mr. THOMAS JOHNSTON, formerly Under Secretary for Scotland, reviewing ' In Search of Scotland,' calls it :

' The most fascinating piece of descriptive writing on a tour in Scotland by an incomer, since old Sam Johnson's " Journey to the Western Hebrides " more than a century and a half ago ; and as a lure for tourists Mr. MORTON could give points even to the author of " Rob Roy." . . . If it be a guide book, then it is the best of its kind ; but it is more, it is enchanted writing which makes the wonderful, beautiful and memorable panorama of our country live again.'

' No recent writer has written so lyrically, picturesquely and freshly of the Romance of Scotland.'—*Sunday Times*.

' What a joyous book it is.'—*British Weekly*.

' Wherever you open it you will find a good story, and plenty of information as well.'—*Spectator*.

' I can think of no traveller's book on Scotland . . . which is so entertainingly and extensively informative.'—Mr. ST. JOHN ERVINE in the *Daily Express*.

IN SEARCH OF IRELAND

With 16 Illustrations and a Map. 7s. 6d. net

'Mr. MORTON has gone in search of Ireland, and has brought home more of it than any other Englishman that I know, because of the range of his interests.'—Mr. S. P. B. MAIS in the *Daily Telegraph*.

'Mr. MORTON's book is an interpretation of the new Ireland, the sketch of an Irish holiday, a guide to Ireland, an impressionist description of country and people, all combined. We do not know of any modern book on Ireland of a like kind which is equal to it in merit. Others, to whom Mr. MORTON acknowledges his indebtedness, have written of things historical, political, literary of Ireland in greater detail, but not with this human touch.'—*New Statesman*.

'If you would know something of the charm of Ireland . . . you must read Mr. MORTON.'—*John o' London's Weekly*.

'Mr. MORTON ranks high in his gift for writing travel books which are works of art.'—Mr. HAROLD NICOLSON in the *Daily Express*.

BOOKS ON LONDON

'Since DICKENS, London has had no truer, more sympathetic interpreter than Mr. MORTON.'—*The Bookman.*

'Mr. MORTON's triumph is that he shows us not only an unfamiliar (or perhaps too familiar) London but also the Londoner.'—*Evening Standard.*

'In "The Spell of London" and its predecessor "The Heart of London," Mr. MORTON has done for the London of to-day what "Sketches by Boz" did for the London of nearly a century ago.'—*The Bookman.*

'Give Mr. H. V. MORTON London as a subject to write about and I know no author to compare with him.'—Mr. RICHARD KING in *Eve.*

3s. 6d. net each

THE HEART OF LONDON
(Also, with Scissor-cuts by L. Hummel, **6s. net**)

THE SPELL OF LONDON
THE NIGHTS OF LONDON
LONDON (The Little Guides series) (**5s. net**)

METHUEN & CO. LTD., LONDON, W.C.2